PRAISE FOR *REAP*

He's done it yet again. I feel like every Mark Sayers book is a must-read, as one's different. Mark aims his brilliant mind, and even more tender heart, not at deconstructing culture as much as reconstructing renewal. Page after page, I felt my heart come alive with hope for the future of the church, and with it, the world. You have to read this one with your soul.

John Mark Comer
Author of *The Ruthless Elimination of Hurry*

If you're trying to make sense of our current cultural landscape and the shape of the gospel within it, here is a message that will electrify you with fresh hope. Mark Sayers is one of the sharpest and most interesting thinkers I know, and *Reappearing Church* is honestly a message for our time. Its insights seem sure to season conversations in cafés, sermons on Sundays, and many of our most passionate prayers for years to come.

Pete Greig
24-7 Prayer International and Emmaus Rd, Guildford, UK

Reappearing Church is a prophetic book of critical importance for our cultural moment. I consistently found myself having to put the book down to have some ime with God, to reorient my heart around a deep longing to see an outpouring f the Spirit that brings revival to the church and an awakening to the culture. If ou long for the same, reading this book will fan the flames in your heart for such n outpouring. Be warned, you probably won't be the same after reading it!

Pete Hughes
Pastor of Kings Cross Church

In my eyes, Mark's understanding of the church and culture today is unmatched. While this book could be yet another voice lamenting how culture negatively affects the church, Mark takes a different approach—showing how our changing times can actually impact the church for the better, if we're willing to fight for a renewal. Mark's solution? Groups of people meeting together who are hungry to move away from "things as they've always been" to reach more people with the good news of Jesus. This is an important book, not only for pastors and church leaders, but also for anyone searching for hope in the church's continued ability to change the world.

Adam Weber
Lead Pastor of Embrace Church and author of *Talking with God*

Mark's new book seized me and shook me as I was slipping into a ministry malaise—deep and disappointed—and said "wake up old preacher, God is not dead, Jesus has not left His church or His world, His Spirit is with us, prepare for revival."

Simon Ponsonby
Teaching Pastor, St. Aldates Oxford

Mark Sayers counters the fragility and failure of secularism with God's renewal pattern arising from living in peaceful presence as we become living temples of His presence. He lays out an eminently livable proposal for partnering with God in renewal by fostering His presence in corporate renewal leading to revival. Don't just read this book. Live it in remnant groups.

Gerry Breshears
Professor of Theology
Western Seminary, Portland, OR, USA

Lately, Christianity in the West has suffered a downward decline due in large part to an emphasis on partisan politics and power as opposed to service, and a posture of strident certainty as opposed to humble love. We are now witnessing the fruit of such misfortunes, namely, a settled belief among our many of our peers that Christianity is not only irrelevant, but possibly even dangerous. In short, the Western church seems to have lost its way. But like every other season of church renewal, minority status and diminishing worship attendance does not necessarily imply a dead Christianity. Rather, it very well might imply a Christianity that is poised for renewal. The tree of God's kingdom, far from being dead, appears to be in a state of pruning for renewed fruitfulness. For anyone desiring to get in on a new work of God, *Reappearing Church* is a most necessary and masterful guide.

Scott Sauls
Senior pastor of Christ Presbyterian Church in Nashville, TN, and author of several books, including *Jesus Outside the Lines* and *Irresistible Faith*

Mark Sayers is one of the most important Christian leaders of our time. Not just because of his brilliant mind that can deconstruct and understand the reality of our current cultural situation, but because he does this with with hope and vision for the way God can work in the chaos and bring restoration through the church. Anyone can tear down, but few are willing to build in the ruins. Mark is one of those leaders, and this book is Mark's wisdom and vision at its finest. *Reappearing Church* is part sociology, theology, and history, but most importantly it is biblical hope for our cynical times. I cannot recommend this book highly enough.

Jon Tyson
Church of the City New York
Author of *The Burden Is Light*

The Hope
for Renewal
in the Rise
of Our
Post-Christian
Culture

REAPPEARING
CHURCH

MARK SAYERS

MOODY PUBLISHERS

CHICAGO

Scripture quotations are taken from the Holy Bible, New International Version®, NIV®. Copyright © 1973, 1978, 1984, 2011 by Biblica, Inc.™ Used by permission of Zondervan. All rights reserved worldwide. www.zondervan.com. The "NIV" and "New International Version" are trademarks registered in the United States Patent and Trademark Office by Biblica, Inc.™

Edited by Connor Sterchi
Interior design: Puckett Smartt
Cover design: Stephen Vosloo and Erik M. Peterson
Cover illustration of rays copyright © 2019 by Farferros / Shutterstock (302325164). All rights reserved.

All websites and phone numbers listed herein are accurate at the time of publication but may change in the future or cease to exist. The listing of website references and resources does not imply publisher endorsement of the site's entire contents. Groups and organizations are listed for informational purposes, and listing does not imply publisher endorsement of their activities.

ISBN: 978-0-8024-1913-2

We hope you enjoy this book from Moody Publishers. Our goal is to provide high-quality, thought-provoking books and products that connect truth to your real needs and challenges. For more information on other books and products written and produced from a biblical perspective, go to www.moodypublishers.com or write to:

Moody Publishers
820 N. LaSalle Boulevard
Chicago, IL 60610

1 3 5 7 9 10 8 6 4 2

Printed in the United States of America

CONTENTS

Creating a Renewal Cell

Our Easter Sunday service had just finished. The finish line of the busiest week in the church calendar. The next morning, not a day off, but an eighteen-hour flight to the US. I was ducking into my office to grab a few things for my journey. Tired, I pulled into the parking lot. Then I saw it. Across the front of our offices was a large sheet and two large words written in spray paint. I got out of my car, looked behind the sheet and there it was. Brazen, bold, and in block letters: "%&$# Off God!"

A note stuck to the wall explained that the sheet (which was blocking the F-bomb) was the charitable work of the Catholic father and some of his church members from the parish across the road. My stomach sank. *Who would do such a thing, on Easter morning of all times?* It felt like the secular moment had reached out with a mendacious targeted message of discouragement. I was already disheartened, concerned by the mood evident in the wider culture. The growing fractious cultural landscape of constant controversy, in which Christianity seemed to be dragged through the mud in continual crisis, at times being targeted, at other times wounding itself. A mood that now reached down into the realities of pastoral ministry, reshaping the inner lives of those I serve for the cause of Christ.

The joy and gratitude that I had felt at the height of our Resurrection

Sunday service dissipated. I was exhausted. I was cold. I just wanted to rest, to spend time with my family before I jumped on the plane.

STOP AND LISTEN

I wondered who I should call to deal with this problem. My staff had already left for their Easter breaks. *Maybe a servant-hearted volunteer?* I pondered. Then, the nudge of the Holy Spirit:

Mark, stop. I want you to deal with this. Paint the wall.

An hour earlier, I had been on stage, preaching to a packed church, and celebrating the resurrection. Now I was grumbling and ferreting around a dark and dusty storage shed looking for a can of paint.

TURNING CURSES INTO BLESSINGS

As I began to paint, my harried, tired state began to slow down as I settled into the gentle and rhythmic brushwork. The sun broke through the clouds, warming the back of my neck. I felt the Spirit nudge me, encouraging me to pray for the person or people who had painted this sign. I asked God to reach out and touch them, reveal Himself to them in their pain and rebellion. The sense that this was an evil secular assault began to disappear. Most likely it was just the work of an angry and bored teenager.

Again, I read the note left by the Catholic priest. I began to marvel that he and his parishioners had spent their Easter morning trying to scrub paint off a concrete wall, locating a sheet to cover the expletive. Something continued to shift in me. Here in this moment of increased antagonism against Christianity, this act of vandalism, this insult to God, had drawn Catholics to serve us, their Protestant brothers and sisters. An Easter moment of grace, a show of Christian unity, that no program or event could manufacture. What other gifts and blessings lay hidden, waiting to be discovered in this secular moment?

Technically, in the parlance of our contested cultural moment, this graffiti could be defined as an anti-religious hate crime. Yet such a viewpoint seemed ridiculous in light of the Christian way Father Dilshan and his parishioners responded. They had merely tried their best to clean up the mess and got on with their worship. I realized that they were driven by a different way of viewing the world—not by fear but rather a desire not to see God's name defamed. Maybe there was a more significant lesson here for the church, I wondered. For in any renewal, God's name is glorified. Curses get turned into blessings.

PAINTING THE SECULAR CANVAS BLANK

After an afternoon's work, the graffiti was gone. In its place a blank wall, but also a blank canvas, covered with fresh paint and fresh possibilities. God had deposited something powerful in me, reframing the challenge before the church in the West. As cultural Christianity washes away, a blank canvas is appearing, with the possibility of a new story being written upon it. What seemed like a crisis, when reframed through the eyes of the Spirit, was an incredible opportunity. Reframed from a lens of defeat to one of potential. God just had to stop me and interrupt my frantic and worried pattern.

In the face of this cultural challenge, our programs, our smarts, our resources, our money, our communications, our skills, our education are not going to cut it anymore. Much of the Western church is operating on the kinetic forward motion of previous moves of God, lounging on a platform built by the service and ministry of passed and passing generations. However, the fuel tank is approaching empty.

What if this secular moment in our culture is only a crisis if we ignore God's calls for renewal? What if we reframe this as brilliantly good news? God always has His people where He wants His people. With nothing to turn to but Him. It is in this place of weakness that His power thunders forth. Do we dare believe that He can do this again in the West?

This book is not written for everyone. I have spoken often and written much in the past for the unsure, the cynical, those with one foot in the world and another in the church. This book, however, I write for those hungry after God. Those desiring to see Him move again with power. Those with a holy discontent. Those who long for His presence to invade their lives, their churches, their cities, and their nations.

We will learn in this book that personal renewal leads to corporate change; we will also discover that God renews His church and culture through a remnant with red-hot faith. My prayer for this book is that it inspires individuals into personal renewal and small groups of believers who will pray and contend for God to move with power through His world.

REFRAMING SECULARISM

As we will discover in the next chapter, many Christians have internalized the secular map of reality. This map continually tells us not to "expect to discover dimensions of reality beyond the empirically evident," Ronald Rolheiser explains, revealing that this assumed secular frame presumes that "the final spiritual exorcism has already taken place. There are no longer any supernatural dimensions to reality, or, in many cases, even to religion."[1] Such a viewpoint is assumed in the West, meaning that it even shapes the assumptions of the believer. Despite our belief in Christ, we can view the decline of the church in the West as inevitable, seeing it through the interpretive lens of the disconnected and detached elites in control of the commanding heights of our media. Interpreters who are stuck in post-Christian thought silos, and therefore have a terrible recent track record on understanding what is happening in our world. Through painting a wall, God changed my viewpoint, causing me to look upon our moment through resurrection lenses. We must examine the possibilities of renewal through God's unlimited power rather than through the limitations of a post-Christian framework, which views the world through a narrow and simplistic materialistic lens, triumphantly expecting the demise of religion and the inevitable victory of Western values.

PATTERN INTERRUPT

That Easter Sunday, God stopped me, interrupting the pattern of life and ministry that was running on autopilot in my life. Like so many of us, I was buzzing around trying to do kingdom business while worrying about the future of the church and the health of our culture. We need to be interrupted. To have our patterns halted. Because doing the same things only delivers the same results.

> ### KEY RENEWAL PRINCIPLE
> **We will not experience renewal by following the same patterns of life and ministry that are not delivering renewal.**

We don't need another book on the challenges that the church faces in the West. We don't need another book to studiously review and critique. We don't need another opinion. We need renewal. So, if you want to be part of a renewal, I want to challenge you to read this book differently—not just to consume more information, but rather to be transformed, joining God in His great renewal project.

We will discover in this book that renewal springs from dedicated small groups. Douglas Hyde understood this principle well. Hyde came to faith in Christ while editor of *The Daily Worker*, the newspaper of the British Communist Party. In 1948, no longer believing that Communism could save the world, Hyde left the political movement he had given his life to and joined the church.

Upon entering the church, Hyde was shocked by what he found, recounting:

*Coming straight, as it were, from one world to another, it astounded me
that there should be people with such numbers at their disposal, and
with the truth on their side, going around weighed down by the thought
that they were a small, beleaguered minority carrying on some sort of
an impossible fight against a big majority. The very concept was wrong.
Psychologically it was calamitous.*[2]

Hyde had left a political movement that, although only containing forty-five thousand members, never saw itself as a fragile minority. Instead, it saw an exciting challenge in their minority position
to be leveraged. Hyde then came to a church, which, although a minority, was far more substantial and better resourced, yet saw itself
through a lens of fragility and defeat.

Hyde encountered a post-war British church, which was struggling in the face of a rising secular threat yet was asking little of its
people and getting little in return. In contrast, the Communist party
that he had left, although wrong in its belief, was able to engender
total dedication in their members. Hyde noted that the Communist
party was filled with Christians who had left their faith, uninspired
by the church's insipid calls upon their lives. "Since so little is asked
of Christians by their leaders, and so much is asked of Communists
by theirs, Christians have small cause for complaint if they seem to
make little impact upon the larger community of which they are
part."[3] Hyde grasped that while Communism was a false gospel, the
church in need of renewal in the West could learn from the ways that
it trained a dedicated minority to renew a culture.

KEY RENEWAL PRINCIPLE
**One person's beleaguered minority is another's dedicated,
committed core. It's all a matter of perspective.**

TRANSFORMATION > INFORMATION, OBEDIENCE > OPINION

Ironically, the training methods used by the Communists were, in fact, closer to those used by the early church than those used by the church of Hyde's day. Michael Green writes that the methods of the early church "stand out in fairly sharp contrast to the procedures most modern churches are disposed to favour."[4] Green notes that while programs, curriculum, or seminary training are helpful, they can also extract students of the gospel from their context. The apostles did not train in a classroom setting; instead, they trained "in the heat of battle and with real encounters." [5]

The Communists that had trained Hyde, like the early church, understood that culture is less taught than caught. This concept applies even to scenarios where information needed to be conveyed. Techniques were employed in which those wishing to learn were thrown into the deep end, where we are forced to learn or flee. One of these techniques was the use of *study groups*—small groups, between three and fourteen, who came together—not for sharing opinions, or for purely social motivations, or for learning some new information that will never be put into practice. Instead, these study groups came together to determine how to be changed, to bring renewal to society. Their goal was to build dedication and leadership into all participants. Their methods of training contained some essential elements:

They looked for and recruited those willing to be trained. They didn't beg people to come. Instead, they recruited the hungry. Prepared for the unreliable and uncommitted to walk away.

They looked for those willing to be changed. The study sessions were not just about information but transformation. Those coming to learn came ready and willing to be renewed for a higher goal.

Up front, they asked for commitment, sacrifice, and a willingness to embrace unpopularity. The Communists were not interested in recruiting the public with slick PR slogans. Instead, they wanted a small committed core. Those coming understood the cost from the get-go.

Students didn't come to be spoon-fed but to become teachers themselves. They understood that we learn best when we have to teach what we are learning. Those coming to study groups would be given a few pages or a chapter of a book of Communist theory to learn before they arrived. Knowing they could be randomly chosen to present, they came prepared to teach the material to the group. This practice turned passive students into active teachers.

Students would be expected each week to put into practice what they were learning. The study groups were not about throwing around opinions but rather obedience to what was being taught. Each lesson would conclude with the question: *How are we going to put this into practice this week?* And each lesson would begin with the question: *How did we put into practice what we learned last week?* Accountability was woven into the structure of the class, which ensured that what was being taught was integrated into people's lives.

THIS IS YOUR PATTERN INTERRUPTION

As we discussed, continuing the same things that are not bringing renewal is not going to bring renewal. Lack of commitment is not going to bring renewal. Business as usual will not bring renewal. Accumulating knowledge without putting it into practice will not bring renewal. We need our autopilot patterns interrupted. You could read this book and learn some things, but is that really going to advance God's dreams of renewal in your life, your church, and your culture?

I want to challenge you with this: one of the most important things you can do is to read this book with a group of people. People you know who are hungry for God's renewal. By doing this, you will create a renewal cell—a small group dedicated to contending for renewal in each other's lives. In your church, your school, your neighborhood, your city, or your nation. The great temptation will be to quickly think of your friends, your social circle, or those you are most comfortable with. But are they the hungriest? Are they those readiest to commit? We need God to reveal who should be in your study group.

So, get out of your chair, stand up and stretch out your hands, or get down on your knees and pray:

God, show me who I can walk this path of renewal with. Lead me to the right people. Place names into my mind.

After praying, names may come to your mind instantly, or it may take a week of prayer or a month. Write your names down below.

WHO WILL I ASK TO MY RENEWAL CELL?

-
-
-
-
-
-
-
-

We will learn more in chapter 12 about how important small groups dedicated to renewal are. One of the key reasons I wrote this book was that I believe that one of the best ways that we can partner with God in His renewal project is to create small groups that are contending for renewal. Yes, a lot of good Christian small groups are out there. Yet in our consumer culture of maximum opinion with minimum responsibility, when all too often our feelings drive our faiths, there are a frightening number of dysfunctional and unfruitful groups.

You can use the guide below to plan your meeting each week in order to grow your study into a renewal cell rather than just another small group or Bible study, to center it on transformation rather than just the accumulation of more information.

- Ensure that those coming understand that this group is not about throwing around ideas or opinions without responsibility. That the purpose of the group is to learn how to commit our lives to God's plan for renewal.

- Meet for a set time (I would recommend one hour). Make an agreement that you will make it your highest priority to attend each meeting. Weak excuses for missing meetings let the group down. I would recommend the no-texting-that-you-are-not-coming rule. It's simply too easy to fire off a lazy text that leaves the burden of responsibility with the rest of your group; instead, call or let others know face to face.

- Meet weekly and communicate to those who you are inviting how long the study will last. Fourteen weeks. Each week will focus upon a chapter. If you don't have fourteen weeks, feel feel to cover two chapters for some sessions.

- Try to guide the discussion away from reading the book; instead, let the book read you. Steer the conversation to how we will work on creating renewal. How we will personally and corporately respond.

- Let people know they need to come prepared. Ready to share a ten- to fifteen-minute compelling summary of the week's chapter. At the end of each chapter, you will find a blank space to write down five concepts or principles that impacted you. If you don't have five principles, that is fine—you may have more or less. What is important is that you have learned the material. Spin a pen to determine who shares each week.

- Always begin with worship. You can choose how you do this. It might be reading, such as a psalm, praise-driven prayer, or musical worship. By starting with the worship of God, we orientate our study around God rather than ourselves.

- Each week we ask how we will put into practice that week what we have learned. As well as asking how we have put into practice what we discovered last week. This element is crucial, ensuring that we are integrating what we are learning, building renewal into our lives.

GROUP SCHEDULE: 1 HOUR

10 minutes – Prayer, worship, and Scripture.

10 minutes – Spin the pen to see who will share a compelling summary of the chapter. If it lands on the same person two weeks in a row, that is just how the cookie crumbles, keeping all group members in a position of readiness to learn.

15 minutes – Group discusses what principle impacted them from this week's reading.

10 minutes – Group explains how they integrated last week's learning, and how this week's learning will be integrated into action and practice during the week.

15 minutes – Contending prayer for God to bring renewal in your personal lives, your church, your neighborhood, your town or city, your school or workplace, your nation, and the world.

WEEKLY GROUP FRAMEWORK: BUILDING A REMNANT

BEGIN WITH WORSHIP – Sing, read a psalm, praise God for what He has done in your lives. Whatever you choose to do, begin by glorifying God. Make this time about Him.

SPIN THE PEN – The person who the pen points to shares their summary of the chapter using the five points below that they prepared earlier as they read the chapter.

WHAT KEY THINGS DID I LEARN FROM THIS CHAPTER?

1.

2.

3.

4.

5.

REFLECTIONS AND GROUP LEARNING – Discuss as a group
What is one renewal principle that you learned in this week's reading? Each person shares one principle that has been discovered.

PARTNERING WITH GOD IN RENEWAL
Share how you each went about integrating last week's chapter into your life and practice. After reflecting on this chapter, what is one personal change you will make this week to partner with God in His plan of renewal? Share with the group, which will keep each other accountable next week.

CONTEND IN PRAYER
What is God asking you to cry out and contend for this week? Contend in prayer for renewal together.

Chapter I

The Secularist Renewal Myth

Presence and Progress on the Road to Renewal

THE CRUDE, STREET-LEVEL SECULAR MYTH

A growing sense of worry haunts the Western church. The rise of a post-Christian society, alongside declining numbers of those who practice biblical faith, combined with a corresponding weakening of Christian influence, has created an anxious mood. This mood can range from a sense of defeat to a feeling of deep vulnerability to a desire to retreat into a religious refuge.

This mood of worry seems justified by the evidence of decline on the ground. However, upon closer examination, this concern is also bolstered by the internalizing of a kind of crude concept of secularism. Ted Turnau notes that most people are not driven by well-understood and articulated philosophical worldviews: "More typically, people express their life philosophy in what we could call a *street philosophy*," which is held intuitively, unexamined, but that powerfully "captures the gist of one's perspective on reality."[1] We see this dynamic at play in popular understandings of secularism. There is a whole field devoted to the study of secularism, yet this body of knowledge rarely trickles down to the average person on the street.

> **The average Westerner processes religion through a crude, street-level model of secularism that is assumed but rarely analyzed.**

This secularist myth centers on the idea that at some undetermined high point of church influence, the West was thoroughly Christian. It is imagined that at this high point, churches were filled with devoted believers and society was filled with Christian values and institutions. This period of strength is usually envisioned as occurring during the Middle Ages, a pinnacle from which the Christian faith has since experienced a decline. If we were to plot such a crude model of secularism on a graph, it would look something like this.

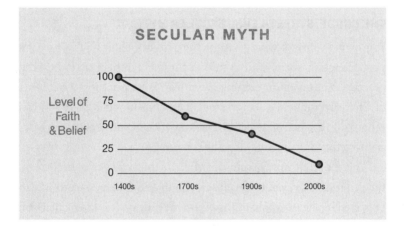

This concept could be described as a kind of street-level myth of secularism, founded on the belief that as we progress in time, we will also advance scientifically, technologically, politically, and morally.

This model presumes that with the right conditions and influences, humans are perfectible and that a kind of human utopia is possible.

All we need is to be educated, informed, and encouraged to progress toward a kind of utopia.

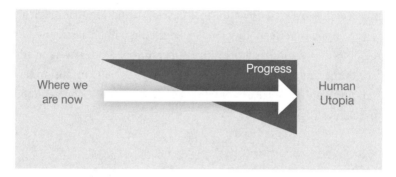

LEFT AND RIGHT ARE BOTH ADDICTED TO PROGRESS

Contemporary culture has become a battleground between left and right. This argument flows into our understanding of faith. The crude secular myth helps us understand the two great political tribes of the West—progressives and conservatives, who both assume its truth.

Progressives are aligned with what is imagined as the inevitable progression toward social utopia and human perfectibility. Conservatives wish to cautiously apply a foot on the brake, conserving the fruits of Western culture while still moving forward. While progressives believe that more government intervention will improve our society, and conservatives believe that the free market will lead us to utopia, they both assume that specific policies can lead us to a free, fair, and prosperous future. Sure, they may squabble over what utopia will look like, but both left and right assume the progress model. Their argument is over the speed at which we should be progressing.

LOSING MY RELIGION

Also undergirding the crude secular myth is a belief that developed among the European philosophical movement of the eighteenth century known as the Enlightenment. This movement developed sophisticated responses to religion and secularism, arguments that few people on the street are familiar with. One Enlightenment belief, however, has trickled down to street level—the notion that the drive toward human perfectibility and social utopia will be accelerated as religion, understood as a primitive superstition, erodes away in the face of the undeniable facts of post-Christian society. In this understanding, faith is seen as something that holds back the assumed march toward progress.

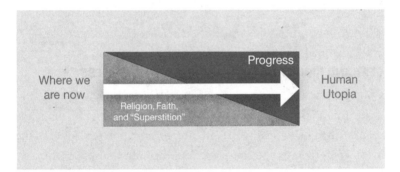

CRUDE SECULARIST APPROACHES TO RELIGION

Today, some still hold to the most radical belief of the Enlightenment, that religion must be destroyed entirely for the world to move forward. This belief gained new oxygen after the attacks of September 11, 2001. The attacks were viewed by the "new atheists" as an attack on Western progress by unsophisticated and backwards religious degenerates, illustrating the danger of faith. Others, confronted with a multicultural and multireligious world, still see a place for religion, but only if it reinterprets its beliefs in light of secularist ideals, and "spiritual knowledge" as personal and privatized "values."[2]

With such thinking dominant among those who control organs of influence in the West, many religious believers assume defeat, seeing religion's only option for survival in submitting to the authority of the secularist script, believing that the only hope for renewal lies in reinterpreting faith around progressive beliefs.

THE CHRISTIAN ORIGINS OF PROGRESS

Like all great myths, the crude secularist myth contains elements of truth. Throughout history, civilizations have made leaps of progress, rapidly advancing as their arts, commerce, philosophy, and influence flourish. Yet such rises are inevitably accompanied by future declines.

> What marks the Western secularist-progressive myth is a religious-like belief that human perfectibility and social progression will continue until we reach utopia.

The secularist-progressive myth asserts that while setbacks occur, eventually there will be an inevitable triumph. Here, the Christian roots of our secularist-progressive myth come into view. This myth mirrors the basic Christian map of reality, with some key differences. The great traditions of the East view history and the world as moving in repeating cycles. In contrast, the Christian view of history sees a linear progression, moving toward a future point of redemption. The West imbibed this linear view. While humans fell in the garden, causing the divine presence to withdraw and bringing sin and destruction into the world, God will triumph at the end of the age with the reconciliation of heaven and earth. His presence will again fill the world.

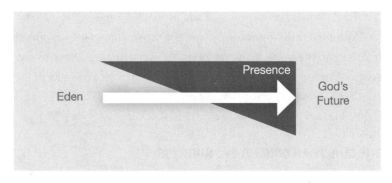

PROGRESS REPLACES GOD'S PRESENCE AS THE ENGINE OF HISTORY

We can see the similarities between the secularist-progressive myth and the Christian understanding of history. The New Jerusalem at the end of the age is substituted for a human utopia. The salvation of humanity by God is supplanted by humans gaining redemption and bliss through their own effort. The historian Christopher Dawson notes that "what is known as the belief in Progress would often be more correctly described as the belief in human perfectibility."[3] Hence, driven by the belief that we can attain perfection without the divine, faith in God gives over to faith in ourselves. Thus the secularist-progressive myth seeks to gain the fruit of God's kingdom—such as justice, peace, prosperity, and redemption—but without the King. Here we arrive at a critical insight that we must grasp as we examine our culture through biblical lenses.

> In the post-Christian vision, progress replaces
> God's presence as the engine of history.

As we will discover, this insight is critical, explaining why so many of our plans as a culture fail. It also sharpens our understanding of why so many of our personal plans also flounder. Looking deeper will also discover that there is another Christian dimension underpinning our secularist-progressive creed.

THE REVIVALIST DYNAMIC

Noting how human culture seemed to progress in bursts and spurts after periods of stagnation, the Scottish minister James Burns observed:

> *Progress, we see, occurs through revival. Any progress is like the incoming tide. Each wave is a revival, going forward, receding, and being followed by another. To the onlooker, it seems as if nothing is gained, but the force behind the ebb and flow is the power of the tide. So it is with nations. One will rise and carry human progress to a zenith. Having done so, it falls back, and another replaces it. Thus, the progress of humanity is continued through successive revivals.*[4]

Burns saw this dynamic occurring throughout human history. He located its origins in God's writing into the fabric of existence a renewal phenomenon, arguing that the revivals that happened in the realm of human culture were mirrors of a spiritual dynamic, in which individuals, communities, and cultures were renewed by the hand of God.

> **KEY RENEWAL PRINCIPLE**
> **God has written a dynamic of renewal into the pattern of history.**

We see this dynamic throughout the history of the church, where small groups of individuals find the church of their age fallen into decline and stagnation, infected by the spirit of the era, heresy, or religiosity. This remnant then seeks to recapture the original dynamism and purity of the apostles' faith. Eventually, this fire catches as God acts with power, reshaping individuals, churches, movements, and whole geographic regions.

WESTERN CULTURE AND THOUGHT IS FILLED WITH REVIVALIST CONCEPTS

We see this revival pattern in the secularist-progressive myth, but it's a kind of Christian revivalism inverted. Enlightenment thinkers, such as Edward Gibbon, looked back to the pre-Christian pagan culture of Rome and Greece in the way that Christian revivalists look back to the witness of the early church, seeing a vibrancy that needed to be recaptured. Many of the philosophical leaders of the Enlightenment saw the West as having fallen into stagnation and decay, not through its embrace of worldliness or heresy, but through its embrace of Christianity.

> In the imagination of the Enlightenment, Christianity was the heresy that had caused Western culture's decline.

RENAISSANCE IS JUST ANOTHER WORD FOR *REVIVAL*

Historian Peter Gay describes the Enlightenment thinkers who shaped our contemporary world as revivalists of the ancient pagan world.[5] Stephen Greenblatt's Pulitzer Prize–winning book, *The Swerve*, sees the origins of our modern, secular, atheistic, and progressive world in the rediscovery of ancient Greek and Roman philosophical texts ignored by Christianity. For the secular revivalists, these texts operate like the New Testament. The rediscovery of these texts created the period of history we call the Renaissance, an Old French term for rebirth or revival.

The nineteenth-century historian Jacob Burckhardt, who popularized the concept of the renaissance, nostalgically looked back to the period, imagining it as the birthplace of a kind of secular golden age that could be rebirthed to operate as a "personal antidote to the violence and discontent of the modern world."[6] Ditching his faith, he reimagined Western history through a kind of secular revivalist framework, a reimagining that influences how we view our story today.

REVIVING THE PERFECT STATE

For key Western thinkers, from Jean-Jacques Rousseau to Thomas Paine, the golden period to return to was not the ancient world of Greece and Rome, but an even earlier period. These thinkers believed that before human society, a pure "natural" state existed—a state in which humans were free of oppression and hierarchy. Paine advocated for "revolutions" that would return us to this pure, primal state of nature, labeling the French and American revolutions as "a renovation of the natural order of things,"[7] illustrating how even the primary political language of the West contains revivalist concepts.

So, to recap: The West's crude secularist-progressive map contains a post-Christian revivalist framework, one in which Christianity itself is the heresy needing to be jettisoned before we can be revived as individuals and as a culture. This map contains a healthy dose of faith, built around the belief that history will end with a human-powered social utopia and the potential of human perfectibility.

Yet this post-Christian revivalist belief is having its own moment of doubt.

DOUBTING THE SECULARIST MYTH

The world that we were promised has not arrived. Well, some of it has appeared. We are more affluent, more technologically connected than ever before in human history. Our technological and scientific knowledge has increased. But have we progressed morally? Thinkers such as scientist Steven Pinker argue we have, that the liberal democratic West is the fairest, most equal, peaceful, and moral sphere to ever exist in human history. Yet at the same time, we see a return of tribalism, a growth in economic inequality, and social divisions expanding. Some speculate that our age will be referred to as the age of genocide. The toxic behaviors of humanity—hatred, bigotry, violence, and selfishness—remain remarkably resilient in individuals, cultures, groups, and nations.

> Post-Christianity is experiencing a crisis of doubt over the prospects of its own program of revival.

MIGRATION IS SHORT-CIRCUITING THE SECULARIST MYTH

Human migration and the reality of a globalized world is also short-circuiting the secularist myth. Religion may be declining in pockets of the West, but it is booming globally, growing in Africa, South America, Oceania, and Asia. Declining birth rates in the West are generating policies of large-scale immigration, which brings migrants into the West, who arrive with their cultures and also their religious faiths.

> Migration is reintroducing faith into the secular bloodstream.

Studying the unexpected return of religion, journalists John Micklethwait and Adrian Woolridge note a sense of exasperation among believers in the eventual triumph of secularism, especially around demography and birth rates: "From Salt Lake City to Jerusalem, religious people marry younger and reproduce more prodigiously than nonreligious ones."[8] For a while, this worry was softened by the belief that eventually, these migrants would secularize as they became immersed in Western culture, and for some that is true. Yet the power of our globally connected world means that migrating to another country is not what it used to be; the internet means one can stay in touch with home, not just socially, but culturally and religiously.

OVERSEAS-BORN YOUNG ADULTS AND FAITH

Research around the values and lifestyles of emerging generations, such as millennials, often used to point toward a more progressive, atheistic future. Yet what is missed is that this is usually only true of Western-born young adults. Evidence of this can be found in my own country of Australia,[9] which has embraced a vigorous policy of multiculturalism and significant large-scale immigration. Indian and Chinese born millennials, two of our current largest migrant groups, are significantly better educated, better savers, more religious, more socially and politically conservative, marry younger, and have more children than locally born millennials. One doesn't need to be a sociologist to predict where this trend will lead.

This helps us understand why political parties on the right, and increasingly on the left, across the West are becoming skeptical about immigration. Concerned that the high fertility rates of migrants, when compared to the disastrously low fertility rates of Westerners, will lead to a future where the secular gains of the West could be lost. Yet it is not just the dynamic between religion and immigration that is causing many to doubt their faith in the progressive-secularist creed.

ROLLING CRISES

The rapid change in the political and social landscape in the last two years across the world has shaken many. A series of rolling crises are exposing human dysfunction, brokenness, and corruption in multiple fields such as Hollywood, the financial sector, Silicon Valley, militaries, big business, politics, sports, and even the church. These crises have naturally created a response, the search for new frameworks of morality. Thus, new programs of progressive morality are being imposed on Western culture, which has for almost a century run from programs of morality. The proponents of this new morality, however, are discovering the same difficulty that religious conservatives in past eras have been confronted by.

Whether it's from the pulpit or the platform of social media, people resent being lectured to. This dynamic creates an expanding and continual culture war, contributing to greater social instability and cultural polarization.

With the rise of powerful nondemocratic leaders in many countries, liberal democracy appears more fragile than a decade ago. A new threat matrix hovers above the international order.

These crises give us a sense that our progression has stalled, in the face of remarkably persistent human failings.

PERSONAL CRISIS

It is not just at the macro level that the secular myth of progress is being challenged. Our private worlds are in crisis too. We see the rise of anxiety and mental health disorders, falling IQ levels, epidemic loneliness and social disconnection, widespread online bullying, and the persistence of discrimination, bigotry, and hatred. Addictions to drugs, food, technology, sex, gambling, and relationships are widespread. Obesity is rising, becoming a full-blown health issue. In the West, poor mental health is now normative among emerging generations. Life expectancy in the West's two most powerful nations, the United States and the United Kingdom, has fallen for the last three years running.[10] With all these factors in play, we can see how many are having their moment of doubt, for the post-Christian revival seems to be running aground.

Chapter 2

The Renewal Pattern

From Holy Discontent to Corporate Revival

THE SECULARIST LIFE SCRIPT IS FRAGILE

The secularist life script, in which humans attempt to live without having to confront the great questions of life, creates insulation against faith. However, this insulation is not as secure as it may seem. For example, during the global financial crisis of 2008, the global banking system came terrifyingly close to a catastrophic worldwide great depression, which would have fundamentally changed the kind of lives we now live. If a major war broke out between great powers such as Russia, China, India, the US, and NATO forces—a threat that many experts agree is increasing—our world and our lives would be radically altered.

If we endured a global flu pandemic, like the one in the early part of the twentieth century that killed millions of people across the world, how we view and process our personal potentials and possibilities would be deeply shaken. Imagine if North Korea launched a devastating cyberattack that disabled most or large parts of the world's internet for months or years. Think about how different your life would be. Consider how you would have to readjust your life and how you access community and relationships.

In Australia, after the attacks on 9/11, church attendance went up for a short period. This was in a country across the other side of the world from the attacks. Why? Because the Western secularist bubble of radical individualism and hyperconsumerism was pierced. Briefly, the mythology that it is possible to live a life without God or greater meaning for many people was rattled.

Your lifestyle, your freedom, your approach to faith and meaning are shaped by large-scale factors. Factors out of our control, which we assume to be stable and secure, but which in reality can change suddenly.

> The secularist life script is dependent on crucial political, economic, and social factors being in place, elements that are becoming fragile, opening a new potential for renewal and revival in the West.

However, before proceeding, we need to examine what exactly we mean by renewal and revival.

RENEWAL: DEFINITIONS AND CONFUSIONS

The terms *renewal, revival,* and *awakening* invoke a variety of emotional responses among Christians. For some, these terms evoke a sense of excitement, corresponding with a pang of hunger to see God move powerfully in our time. For others, such words belong in the dusty annals of church history, appreciated but distant from our secular moment, where decline rather than renewal seems the norm.

Others will hear these terms with a sense of apprehension, their minds filled with images of hype-driven worship services, endlessly repeated choruses, and the exhaustion of never-ending church activity. So it's vital to establish the way in which these terms will be used in this book.

Church history often uses the terms *renewal, revival,* and *awakening* interchangeably. *Revival* is used to describe what happened during the eighteenth century in Britain, whereas in the United States, the term *awakening* is often used. Both labels are used to describe the same move of God that occurred in different places. So, in this book, I am going to use these terms in the following ways:

Renewal:

A) The refreshment, release, and advancement that individuals, groups, churches, and cultures experience when they are realigned with God's presence.

B) The resumption of our God-given purpose to partner with God fully, participating in His plan to flood the world with His presence.

Revival:

When renewal occurs on a large scale, bringing significant advancement, growth, and kingdom fruit to a city, people group, movement, region, or nations. Revival is renewal gone viral.

THE PROCESS OF RENEWAL IS BUILT INTO THE WORLD

We learned in the previous chapter that renewal is built into the fabric of our world. Since the fall, God has been in the renewal business. We intuitively sense this. Everybody understands that something is wrong in the world and desires a better future. We hope that our lives and our cultures are better tomorrow than they are today. We naturally try and move toward renewal.

We either yearn for renewal or lament its absence.

Yet without God, our flesh-driven renewal programs, both personal and corporate, will bring more harm than good. When it comes to renewal, we face four options:

HUMAN-DRIVEN RENEWAL: To renew in our own human strength.

STAGNATION: To attempt to press pause, ignoring renewal, while trying to avoid decline.

DECLINE: To resist renewal, thus sliding into decline.

GOD-CENTERED RENEWAL: To align with God's plan to renew us and the world.

RENEWAL IS GOD'S TOOL TO MOVE HISTORY TOWARD HIS ENDS

God is intent on partnering with humans in His plan to redeem the world. As we will discover, God is profoundly relational. He created you to spread His presence into the world. When we rejected this call upon us, He gave His Son, Jesus, on the cross so that we would again pick up this mandate.

Because God is relational and intent on inviting us into His mission in the world, He primarily uses the pattern of renewal to realign us with His purposes.

RENEWAL FLOWS THROUGH SYSTEMS

Renewal is God's way of cleansing and reviving the systems in which we exist and operate. Often we approach our challenges by imagining a future vision of what renewal looks like, and then we take off toward that goal. However, organizational theorist Peter Senge observes that "vision without systems thinking ends up painting lovely pictures of the future with no deep understanding of the forces that must be mastered to move from here to there."[1] When we just have a vision-based approach to renewal, the ends can justify the means. In God's way of renewal, our systems in their entirety, both personal and corporate, must be renewed for us to be moved forward. (We will learn more about this crucial distinction in chapter 4.)

GOD LEADS IN THE DANCE OF RENEWAL, YET WE MUST BE GOOD PARTNERS

One of the great questions that swirl around renewal and revival concerns God's sovereignty. Do they occur only at His will and whim? Or is there anything we can do to make them happen? I believe that God chooses when and where He will move. I also believe that God is looking for a people amongst whom He can dwell. His kingdom comes to those who hunger and thirst after His righteousness. Therefore, throughout history, we observe a pattern. When we cry out to Him, when we repent of the ways that we have ignored Him and pursued our human-driven plans of renewal in our own strength, when we take a posture of contending for His kingdom to come with power—we see that He moves.

> ### KEY RENEWAL PRINCIPLE
> God chooses when, where, and whom He will renew.
> Yet we can prepare for His coming.

We don't get to choose how He moves, yet the biblical record and church history prove the words of God in 2 Chronicles 7:14—that He moves when His people humble themselves, praying and seeking His face while turning from their sin. This illuminates a fundamental renewal principle.

KEY RENEWAL PRINCIPLE
Often the biggest blockage to renewal is ourselves.

Therefore, when it comes to renewal, God leads the dance. He controls the significant elements of renewal—the pouring out of His Spirit and presence with power and force, the wholesale transformation of communities, cities, and nations. Yet God did not create us as robots, but rather as partners. For we can prepare for the dance, making ourselves ready to be led. We can ensure that our feet don't get in the way, or that we don't try and lead the dance.

We cannot create a program or campaign for renewal and revival. For in the history of the church, this has rarely if ever had success. Instead, we can humbly align ourselves with the pattern that God uses to renew us and our systems.

We discover in renewal that God gives us freedom and latitude to instigate small changes that create an environment in which He enjoys to partner with His children.

PERSONAL RENEWAL LEADS TO CORPORATE RENEWAL

Trace a revival back to its origins and you will inevitably find a person or a handful of people moved by God. People who God took on a renewal process that first changed them before it changed others. They experience a microcosm of revival. Usually this process happens to people who are not necessarily the leader everyone is expecting to be used powerfully in a move of God. Instead, the process of renewal remolds them for God's purpose. Almost always this renewal will occur in hidden places of obscurity, in a period of isolation, in which deep roots are grown for the influence that is to come, and resilience and perseverance built for the resulting challenges.

KEY RENEWAL PRINCIPLE
Personal renewal precedes corporate renewal.

All of us are called to walk the process of renewal called discipleship. Stepping into the personal renewal that God wishes for us is the surest lever for influencing a church, a family, or an organization toward His purposes.

RENEWAL ALIGNS US WITH GOD'S SOVEREIGN TIME

There is no guarantee that if we follow God's pattern, a large-scale revival will break out. The pattern is not a guaranteed formula. While I believe that we must obey God's pattern of renewal, which will see the production of kingdom fruit, there is no promise that by aligning ourselves with it, we will see spectacular growth. Dismayed by the affluence and the lack of faith in my hometown of Melbourne, small groups of Christians began to pray for my city in the late 1850s. They persevered in prayer until God began to move with power, and thousands came to faith.

The origins of the church I lead can be traced back to this revival when the American evangelist R. A. Torrey, D. L. Moody's ministry partner, came to Melbourne to conduct a series of evangelistic meetings. Yet this breakthrough did not occur in its full strength until fifty years later, breaking with full force at the beginning of the twentieth century in 1902. Many of those who prayed fervently for Melbourne to see revival never lived to see the results of their prayers.

KEY RENEWAL PRINCIPLE
When it comes to renewal, we must align with
God's timetable.

We accept that the role He has for us might be to contend for a move amongst a future generation. However, we also contend and pray that He will move in our time, submitting to His will and wisdom as to how He wishes to move.

THE NEXT GREAT AWAKENING?

The Methodist theologian Albert C. Outler, speculating in the early 1970s, noted that the church could not have another Great Awakening until we realized that the second Great Awakening, which revived the church in the late eighteenth and early nineteenth centuries, was over.[2] The second Great Awakening was a powerful response by God to a unique cultural moment that was shaking and reshaping the world. We face a similar moment of upheaval, but with crucial differences. We need God to pour out His Spirit on the particular challenges we are facing in this moment in which we live.

WE WILL FOCUS ON BUILDING A FOUNDATION FOR RENEWAL

Therefore, strategically, I am not going to spend much time discussing elements such as missional practice, social justice, church planting, or cultural engagement, which are components that many readers will see as essential to the renewal of the Western church. This is not because I do not believe that these elements are crucial to renewal. I believe in them all. This book, however, is a response to a particular trend that is of unparalleled importance. Over the last ten years, I have seen countless incredible kingdom initiatives suffer and fail as leaders and disciples, with hearts for God, fall into error, sin, stagnation, heresy, religiosity, or all of the above. Why?

> Our current Western context deforms our hearts and lives in profoundly destructive ways.

Big Business, Big Data, and Big Porn's ability to reshape our inner worlds is unparalleled in human history. I have cried enough tears while seeing amazing initiatives for God fail as the disorder of our human hearts, exacerbated by our cultural scripts, shreds good intentions and eviscerates holy dreams. Therefore, the next Great Awakening, the next renewal, the coming revival, must be centered on our hearts being changed by God. It must begin by replacing the pseudo-Christianity of lifestyle enhancement with the Spirit-filled faith of biblical Christianity. It must offer the renewal of Christlikeness to those being deformed by our culture in the deepest parts of their hearts.

> **We need a new generation of Christians engaged in mission, kingdom vocational living, cultural engagement, and biblical justice—filled with His Spirit, formed by the way of Jesus, and shaped by heavenly wisdom.**

So, this book will front-end its exploration of renewal, offering insights into how God changes individuals and small groups of people to offer a holy foundation upon which greater expansions of renewal can proceed. As Tim Keller notes of renewal, "It is a consistent pattern of how the Holy Spirit works in a community to counteract the default mode of the human heart."[3] Our exploration going forward will focus on how God can do this in our cultural moment, for renewal always begins with the human heart. We will explore the process God uses to renew us first, and then the relationships around us.

THE RENEWAL PROCESS

Understanding these key concepts, we can now get an overview of the renewal pattern. As we examine the history of revivals, the biblical basis, and the literature on renewal, we begin to see an essential design. At the heart of this process is God's desire to renew us and our life systems, to use His presence to align us with His purposes, and to release us into our God-given mandate for which He created us. The renewal pattern is composed of four stages through which we progress: **Holy Discontent**, which leads into **Preparation**, which then sets us up for the posture of **Contending**, which then moves into the formation of **Patterns** that center our lives around God's presence. A group of people gathered around this process then finds each other, forming a **Remnant**. The process looks like this, moving in a clockwise direction.

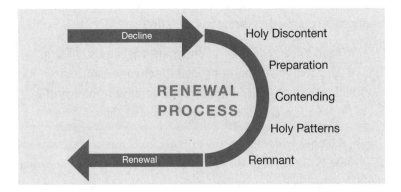

The remainder of the book will be spent exploring how this pattern works and how we can align with God's process of renewal. But first, a quick overview to understand the territory we will be traveling through.

PHASE I: HOLY DISCONTENT

Deep dissatisfaction with the low state of our faith, the church, and the culture.

The first phase of renewal is Holy Discontent. Here, the dismay between the hunger for something better and the reality in which we are living coalesces from frustration or lament into a holy discontent. Our desires begin to align with God's desire to renew the world. In the phase of Holy Discontent, we become ***discontent with the state of*** *the world,* perceiving its injustices, sinfulness, brokenness, and lostness. Its failings become painfully real to us. Often this is facilitated by a personal or corporate crisis, which brings our lives into a new light.

We become *discontent with the state of the church,* but not in a critical nitpicking sense. Instead, we experience a genuine hunger for the church to be released into its full potential and power in our broken world. These discontents then ferment into a deep *dissatisfaction with the state of our own lives* and the level of our own faith. No longer pointing fingers of accusation outward, we realize our own inadequacy. Grasping that change must begin with us; instead of falling into self-condemnation or paralysis, we cry out to God to change us, to start His renewal in our hearts.

PHASE 2: PREPARATION

The deep work of preparation that God undertakes in the hearts of those He wishes to fill with His presence.

Our Holy Discontent then becomes so powerful that we cannot go on any longer, we cannot tolerate the state of our lives, of the church, or of our culture. The next step forward is not a program of renewal, nor a campaign for change. Instead, it is lived in the hidden places, in obscurity, often drenched with tears. Built on late nights or early mornings, quiet spaces with His Spirit and His Word. Calling out for God to first begin with us. For, as my friend Joshua Ryan Butler says, "The heart of the problem is the problem of the heart."[4] Thus, renewal must begin with the preparation of our hearts. We experience the stages of this phase as God renews and realigns our hearts. God brings *conviction*—how we fall short of His standards is revealed. We begin to compare ourselves, not sideways against peers or culture, but to God's eternal holiness. Not only do the things we do wrong come into focus, but also the good things we are not doing.

We then move into a *fight against the flesh,* in which we begin to remove the obstacles to renewal that exist in our hearts, allowing God to change our habits, desires, and attitudes. This primarily occurs through the process of **confession and repentance.** By following Scripture's command to confess to our fellow believers, making right relationally what was wrong. Examining our life and our kingdom walk through the King's standards, and repenting of the way that we have fallen short. For the heart of repentance is *metanoia*, the decision to turn around the direction of our lives and walk in step with His voice.

PHASE 3: CONTENDING

The act of moving from a life posture of consumption and passivity to one of contending for God's presence to come with power.

With prepared hearts, we now step into the phase of contending. Contending means to stretch, or fight for something. We come to the point where we realize that our lives, our faith, our churches, and our culture cannot be changed by anything else but the presence of God. We wish for nothing but His presence, and so we position and posture ourselves as contenders for His presence. Following the words of God in Ezekiel, we choose to stand in the gap for our culture, crying out for God's mercy, asking Him to come again.

This occurs through the shift of **contending prayer,** which is common in all moves of God. Individuals or small groups of people cry out for God to move, seeking God's will on earth as it is in heaven. This kind of prayer is almost always persistent, as God uses the passage of time to shape us, realigning us to His timescale, teaching His people the value of **persistence**, a vital element of those He wishes to use in renewal.

PHASE 4: HOLY PATTERNS

Reorienting our life around patterns that enable us to live and operate in God's presence.

Patterns of *formation* begin to take shape. Practices and habits that help us live vital Christian lives, focusing on the power of God's presence, become essential. These patterns become an alternative to the world's great models of formation. These patterns center the rhythms of our lives around God's presence. These are spiritual disciplines that have shaped the church throughout the millennia—prayer, the reading of Scripture, the contours of communal Christian faith.

PHASE 5: THE REMNANT

A group of individuals being renewed by God come together to contend for God to move powerfully.

Individuals come together to contend. Small groups of contending prayers begin to emerge into a *remnant* of renewed believers, hungry for God to move, discovering forgotten habits and practices that have nourished and nurtured the people of God through the church's history. These practices and habits are infused with a new vibrancy and power as the presence moves amongst those seeking Him. The foundations for a move of God are established.

PHASE 6: RENEWAL

As God moves, new life flows into the person or people of God. New vitality breaks out; the person or people walk with God in His presence, empowered by Him. His *presence comes with power*. Ministry is *quickened and empowered*. What was excruciatingly slow and challenging before is now accelerated, as ministry is powered not by human effort but by His presence. The individual, church, culture, or movement, centered around God, now moves into a time of *growth and advance* as the kingdom moves forward, refreshing His people and those around them. Refreshment flows outward as the church becomes the ambassador of His presence in the world.

PHASE 7: REVIVAL

Renewal goes viral, spreading across churches, regions, cities, denominations, and countries. The church is significantly advanced, ground is taken for the gospel, and positive change builds a new foundation of health and kingdom fruit.

Chapter 3

Crisis—The Gateway to Renewal

The Silver Lining to Be Found in Dark Clouds

TRANSITIONS ARE GATEWAYS TO RENEWAL

The concept of transitions is essential to understanding renewal. George Hunter, writing of the potential for renewal in the secular West, notes that when it comes to openness to the gospel, "persons experiencing important life transitions are more receptive than persons in stable periods of life." Such transition "tends to 'unfreeze' their lives and makes change possible."[1] Individuals in the midst of a life transition are thus more open to the gospel. Transitions open up new potentials for renewal. They move us into a new phase, opening up the possibility of renewal. This is true not just of the unbelievers of whom Hunter was writing, but also for those of us who hunger for renewal.

KEY RENEWAL PRINCIPLE
Renewal follows periods of crisis, change, and transition.

As we study how God brings renewal throughout history, we begin to see the pattern that crisis plays in renewal. A community may experience a natural disaster or war and be pushed back into God. An individual may experience a period of wilderness and isolation, crying out to God, who then comes to them in their pain. This person gains spiritual depth, being renewed, becoming an influencer for God.

Crises, and the transitions that they bring, are one of the critical ways that God uses to move us. Organizational consultant William Bridges observed that transitions are different than mere change. Mere change is simply a switch of circumstances, whereas transitions affect us profoundly at a psychological and emotional level. Bridges notes that transitions contain three phases:

1. *Letting go of the old ways and the old identity people had. This first phase of transition is an ending, and the time when you need to help people to deal with their losses.*
2. *Going through an in-between time when the old is gone but the new isn't fully operational. We call this time the "neutral zone": it's when the critical psychological realignments and repatternings take place.*
3. *Coming out of the transition and making a new beginning. This is when people develop the new identity, experience the new energy, and discover the new sense of purpose that make the change begin to work.*[2]

Transitions must be navigated carefully with wisdom. They are potential gateways to renewal, opportunities to turn back to God, to move deeper into Him. Terry Walling writes, "Transitions serve to bring about needed change, provide clarity in life direction, consolidate learning, deepen values, shift paradigms, and advance one's influence and/or ministry."[3]

Transitions force us to align ourselves to Him and His purposes. Yet transitions also operate as gateways of possibility. As with any gateway, we can choose not to pass through them. Transition gateways are often the places where people get blocked, stagnate, or turn back. It is crucial that in the renewal pattern we see the importance of transitions in moving between phases.

> During transitions, God offers us the chance to go
> deeper with Him.

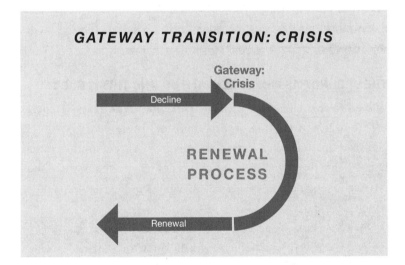

GATEWAY TRANSITION: CRISIS

The rawest form of transition is a crisis. It is the surest antidote to complacency. John P. Kotter, recognized as one of the world's leading experts on managing change, notes the role that crises play in fostering positive change, even advising that "real leaders often create . . . artificial crises rather than waiting for something to happen."[4] One might wonder if we need to follow this advice to advance change in the West. Don't worry; as we will learn, contemporary culture is doing fine creating its own crisis.

THE WORLD IS ENTERING A TRANSITION

What we are experiencing in this moment of cultural upheaval and change is a series of significant and substantial transitions, affecting not just individuals but also nations and cultures. The West, and indeed the world, is entering a transition, and as Bridges notes above, this means that old ways of understanding come to an end. We can be in a transition without having the language to describe it. We can also be in a state of denial that a transition is occurring. Those who are most invested in the passing period fail to notice its passing and that transition has begun. We can also experience a sense of loss as we enter transitions, grasping that something has ended. These are signs we are coming to the first stage of this transition.

THE GROUND HAS MOVED BENEATH US, AND THIS IS GOOD

Wilbert Shenk noted that "the Christian faith has been saved repeatedly in nearly two thousand years of history by moving from an established heartland to a new environment."[5] The cultural transition we are living through has placed us in a new environment without us physically moving. The contested, changing culture is a new land in which we find ourselves.

To many, such a time as this seems foreboding, unknown, and unsafe. If we measure what is happening through the metrics of success the world offers, it can seem worrying. Yet, examining our moment through spiritual lenses, we will discover this transition opens up all kinds of new possibilities.

The idea that this new place where we find ourselves could be hopeful seems counterintuitive. Yet a study of history shows that it is precisely at moments like this—when the church appears to be sliding into an unalterable decline, when culture is shaken by upheaval, when the world globalizes, opening up new frontiers and fostering chaos and change—that God moves again.

KEY RENEWAL PRINCIPLE
Revivals and renewals always come at low
ebbs of church and culture

Faith has not slowly ebbed away during the centuries. Instead, renewal is replaced by stagnation, which mutates into decline, and which eventually returns to renewal.

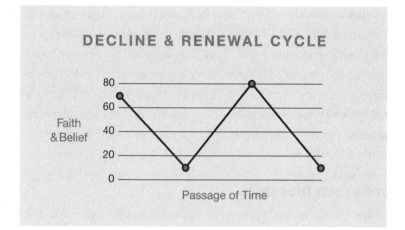

James Burns, in his study of revivals throughout the history of the Christian church, notes that times of dismay about the state of faith and the church should be reframed, reminding us that "this time of spiritual deadness has its definite limits. The wave of spiritual progress recedes, but in receding it is gathering in power and volume to return, and to rush further in. God has set a limit to the defection of His church. When the night is at its darkest, the dawn is on the way."[6] We find ourselves again at such a moment.

> ### KEY RENEWAL PRINCIPLE
> To human eyes, the tide seems to have retreated, but out beyond the breakers, the power is growing, churning in hiddenness, preparing to return with force.

The secularist-progressive creed is looking weaker than it initially appeared. The gaps between its promises and reality are widening. Its contradictions are being revealed in increasingly plain sight, causing significant cultural upheaval and change: rising inequality between rich and poor; distance between elites and everyday people; the growth of loneliness and social disconnection despite our hyper-connection; a burgeoning crisis of meaning despite our affluence; the increase in social fracture and conflict; the disruptive effect of technology upon our environment, our health, and social sphere; the growing threat of full-scale war and nuclear conflict in our multipolar world.

CHRIST IS IN THE CRISIS

Before us is a unique moment of opportunity. God's presence is at work behind much of our cultural chaos. Our culture seeks a secularized version of renewal, attempting to live without God's presence. Yet in reality, it is experiencing God's presence. It is there as a form of judgment. Lebanese Christian thinker Charles Malik asks of us:

> *Are you perplexed? Do you "feel" the crisis? Do you "feel" something profoundly wrong, both in your life and in the affairs of the world? Do you as it were "hold your heart in your hand," fearing that at almost the next moment something terrible is going to break out*—both in you and the world? *Have you reached the state where you simply do not quite trust the processes of the world (including nature, science, economics, politics, and even the best good will), suspecting that there*

is in them a flaw somewhere, a false note, an immanent principle of darkness, destruction, and death?[7]

We all sense this swirl of chaos in our time, we see the crisis all around us. Yet Malik then says something both shocking and profound, that "at its deepest levels, the crisis is *caused* by Christ." This great cultural tumult, this crisis in the world, is "simply the fact that Jesus Christ is the Lord and is judging."[8] Malik rightly identifies that the profound crisis that both individuals and societies are experiencing in the world is because Christ's presence has now gone out into the world and His presence brings judgment.

> Our cultural crises show us the consequences of what happens when we try and take over the controls of the world.

To the contrite of heart, the humble, the meek in spirit, God's presence is received as waves of love. Yet for the proud, the rebellious, the autonomous, the individuals and systems that wish to continue Adam and Eve's rebellion to reanimate the project of Babylon, to reach for progress without presence—for such people and systems, those same waves of love that are God's presence are experienced as judgment.

SECULARISM AS JUDGMENT

Lesslie Newbigin saw God using the crisis caused by secularism as part of His judgment in the world. After Christ had humiliated the power and principalities upon the cross, the sacred orders of the world were exposed. It was either God's unmediated presence or nothing.

Of secularism, Newbigin could say, "As a Christian I see this process of secularisation as an extension of the prophetic attack, in the name of the living God, upon all structures of thought, patterns of society, idols whether mental or metal, which claim sacred authority."[9] It's an important argument. Newbigin was arguing that Christ was using the power of secularism against itself to undermine all forms of belief in the world. As humans attempted to live without God, every-thing would fall in on itself. We see this in our time, as the corruption at the heart of so many industries and sectors of culture is revealed. As secular people push toward cultural, moral, and political renewal, they only expose more brokenness and sin. Our culture lurches from attempts at renewal to reaction and back again in a feverish sickness.

All programs of progress, without the presence, create chaos and crisis.

Secularism's attempt to attack all sacred orders, and live without belief, ultimately leads to exhaustion, a lack of meaning that throws it back into a religious impulse. Writing in the midtwentieth century, Newbigin predicted that the West would return to the extremes of politics as religion—a move we can see in our day. This in turn only leads to more chaos, exhaustion, and disillusionment as the West continues to fail at its projects of renewal. In this exhaustion and dis-order, we see the hand of God's merciful judgment, which allows us to rest on nothing but His presence. He has inserted a Babel-like kill switch inside of human endeavors without Him. Nothing and no one can truly advance a program of renewal without His presence.

God allows cultural crises to drive us back to Him.

In the chaos of our Western cultural system, we see God's presence at work. We must view what God is doing in our world through the lens of His presence, bringing our life systems under the judgment of His presence. The failures we see in our societies, structures, and sys-tems, their inability to truly deliver what our hearts desire, illuminate their incapacity to replace God. Their failings illustrate God's judg-ment upon them and anything that attempts to operate apart from Him. We see this concept at play in Joel 2, as the prophet describes the return of the presence of God to Jerusalem as akin to a horde of locusts, devouring that which opposes God, devastating the corrupt social, religious, and political systems that occupied the holy city.

BURNING THE BOATS

Upon landing in Spain in the eighth century, the Arabic military commander Tariq was vastly outnumbered. Realizing this, he did something counterintuitive, ordering his troops to burn their boats, an act that would incinerate their only insurance policy. Gathering his men, he told them, "Behind you is the sea, before you, the enemy. You are vastly outnumbered. All you have is sword and courage."[10] There was no other option left but to throw everything into the fight.

The Chinese sage of strategy Sun Tzu also advocated for the burning the boats to establish what he called "death ground." That is the desperate place where you either fight or die. Burning the boats is the ultimate motivational tool. For with the boats burned, there can be no observers, no divided loyalties. There are no critics on death ground. There are only two choices: do or die.

The strategy of burning the boats is ultimately a human one, a way of squeezing the maximum motivation out of humans. We have been placed on a kind of death ground—our boats have been burned. The sheer scale of the cultural challenge before us, the way our culture is able to shape and form us at deep levels, means that we are on death ground whether we realize it or not. A church and a faith built upon the framework of radical individualism can only last so long.

> The church in the West is at a renew or decline moment.
> Our cultural crisis is burning our boats for us.

By continuing with the status quo, we plug ourselves into the anti-renewal machine. Business as usual, the satiating of consumer Christianity, the mere provision of pleasing religious goods and services, will see us infected and eventually die of the toxicity in the system of the culture. However, as culture burns our boats, we can say to Jesus with the apostle Peter, "Lord, to whom shall we go? You have the words of eternal life" (John 6:68).

Chapter 4

From Dissatisfaction to Holy Discontent

Ripe for Renewal in the Ruin of Meaninglessness and Unlimited Freedom

THE FERTILE GROUND OF DISSATISFACTION

At the height of Hollywood's golden age, Howard Hughes was everywhere. Plastered all over the gossip pages, he was the midcentury embodiment of a glamorous celebrity. Someone who drunk lustily from the well of personal freedom that the modern world offered. An Academy Award–winning Hollywood producer, property baron, daredevil pilot, and breaker of land speed records. He was tall, handsome, and smashingly rich. Hughes dated scores of Hollywood's most desired women. He was a walking advertisement for the freedoms of technology, sex, money, and power offered by the modern world.

Hughes's later years would be anything but an expanse of freedom. At some point during his forties, Hughes disappeared into darkened rooms within hotels he owned, becoming a recluse. Blocking out the world, he retreated into the screen, a movie projector in his room allowing him to endlessly binge on his favorite films while he filled his body with codeine. A telephone line, his only communication with the outside world. The man who embodied the freedom and movement of the modern world, now paralyzed by the screen. Oppressed and imprisoned by his appetites, pleasure and power gave way to paranoia and suffocating anxiety.

Hughes is a symbolic figure. With the first half of his life, he showcased the promise of our unlimited freedom, but in the second half of his life, he became a different of kind of pioneer, showing us the destination of unlimited freedom. His imprisonment in front of the glow of the screen, anxiety his only companion, his spiritual vacuum soothed by opioids, now reads as descriptive of the kind of excesses the media worries have become all too prevalent in contemporary culture. It shows us the discontent that grows from unlimited freedom.

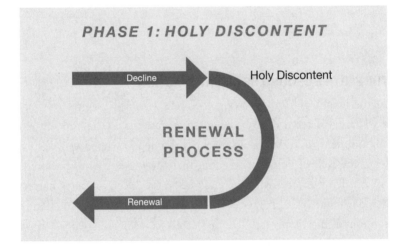

PHASE 1: HOLY DISCONTENT

Decline · Holy Discontent · RENEWAL PROCESS · Renewal

As the gap between what our culture promises and what it delivers grows wider, its failures create openings for the gospel. Idols are shown for what they are—new potentials open up for God to again move.

George Hunter notes that it is not only people in transitions who are receptive to the gospel,[1] but also those experiencing a sense of dissatisfaction with the outcome of their lives. Transition and dissatisfaction often are companions. James Burns saw the period before a renewal as a time of growing dissatisfaction and discontent.[2]

This sense of growing dissatisfaction in our time is growing in proportion to the promises of our Western consumerist culture, which has promised to deliver us both social and personal utopia. Previous ages understood that happiness and lasting pleasure might be elusive, yet we now inhabit a media-drenched landscape in which endless promises of improvement accompany us throughout our lives. These promises are a post-Christian vision of personal renewal. Emptied of the transcendent, we now reach for reduced visions of the good life, from the quest for physical health to the quest for safety and emotional security in an increasingly risky world.

POST-CHRISTIAN PERSONAL RENEWAL

Psychologist Dan P. McAdams notes that the Christian shape of individual redemption has remained, but its content has been replaced with secular elements.[3] This secular salvation is found now in what Philip Cushman described as "the lifestyle solution," which was the answer to the problem of "the empty self."[4] Modern culture, relentlessly undermining foundations of meaning, creates an inner emptiness, an inner life in constant need of repair, and salvation. The elements of the post-Christian personal renewal are as follows:

1) *We are born innocent, happy, and whole. Our inner child or inner self is good.*

2) *Families, bad experiences, binding commitments, externally given identities, cultural, traditional, and religious restrictions make us unhappy, giving us low self-esteem.*

3) Through escaping from these binding commitments, externally given identities, traditions, and religious restrictions, we discover our inner self, which is good and can guide us.

4) Through finding a missing element such as a soulmate, meaningful career, enjoyable experiences, material things, or through exercising our self-expression, our lives can be filled with pleasure and meaning.

Our consumer-shaped culture then offers us endless promises to fill our "empty selves," which it creates in the first place.

Contemporary consumer culture offers medicine to cure the diseases it creates.

Reflecting on this culture of promise, anthropologist Thomas De Zengotita warns that "there is no going back to reality." Social media and emerging technologies have made this place immersive, therefore, "We have been consigned to a new plane of being . . . a place where everything is addressed to us, everything is for us, and nothing is beyond us anymore."[5] This is the culture of superabundance, which doesn't simply promise a life of comfort and opportunity but also offers a never-ending parade of consumer goods and experiences. Older forms of consumerism required the individual to travel to stores or malls in search of satisfaction. This next stage of intensified consumerism comes to us, in the form of home delivery, downloads, and streaming, all increasing the strength of our individualism.

We cannot escape from the promise that we can have it all. We also cannot escape from the truth that we can't have it all.

THE PROMISES OF PERSONAL RENEWAL ARE FALLING FLAT

The promises of our cultural and political elites that things will get better are falling flat. We have endless opportunities to pursue pleasure and our desires, yet so many of us are miserable and anxious. We can traverse geography, time, and space, yet loneliness is growing. Silicon Valley's promises that a world connected by social media will be a better, more tolerant world now look ridiculous. The assurances that a globalized world will be a fairer, more peaceful and prosperous place seem shaky. These failed promises are fuelling a growing sense of dissatisfaction, a desire to see things change, a hunger for a vision of personal and social life in which humans flourish.

A FLOURISHING SYSTEM

In Psalm 1 we are given an image of what human flourishing looks like:

> Blessed is the one
>   who does not walk in step with the wicked
> or stand in the way that sinners take
>   or sit in the company of mockers,
> but whose delight is in the law of the LORD,
>   and who meditates on his law day and night.
> That person is like a tree planted by streams of water,
>   which yields its fruit in season
> and whose leaf does not wither—
>   whatever they do prospers.

The psalm offers us a model of what faithful and fruitful living looks like. Michael Wilcock notes that the vision it paints of the good life is a challenge to "the whole range of modern-isms, from liberalism to post-modernism, which shy away from the notion of objective truth and error, right and wrong. . . . It challenges the individual to repeated choices between clearly defined ways of believing and acting."[6] Such a vision of the good life contrasts with the fuzzy drift toward utopia we see in the secularist-progressive myth, instead offering us a definitive model in which we are all invited to live.

> ### The use of a model from the natural world—a tree planted by water, bearing fruit in season—reveals to us a definitive and binding way to live.

There is no way for any human or society to truly and wholly flourish without following this model.

The final verse of the psalm also reminds us that those who do not follow this model will find themselves and their endeavors leading to destruction. We are given in this psalm a path to flourishing that contains a vital truth about the world. That we live in systems, and our dissatisfaction or, indeed, satisfaction in life flows from the health of the systems in which we live in. A gnawing sense of resentment and discontent, and an accompanying failure to flourish, is a sure sign the system of Western culture is failing and ill.

WE LIVE IN SYSTEMS

Regarding Christ's role in creation, Paul writes to the Colossians, "For in him all things were created: things in heaven and on earth, visible and invisible, whether thrones or powers or rulers or authorities; all things have been created through him and for him" (Col. 1:15–16). The Greek word used to describe the reality that all things have their being in Him is *synhesteken*, from which we get our English word *system*. As theologian Hendrick Berkhof notes, this means that Christ is the system that holds the universe and all of creation together.[7] Two crucial truths come into view. First, that everything exists in an interconnected system, and second, that Christ is at the center of that system.

We can describe our culture as a vast, mysterious force. We try to understand its history and its construction, to see why it is the way it is, and predict where it could move next.

A better lens with which to understand our culture, and the role of revival and renewal in human history, is to realize that we live in a system.

Understanding our culture as a system is liberating; not only does it help us grasp its shape, but also its effectiveness. The concept of systems can initially seem complicated, but in reality, it is a simple idea that we intuitively understand because we spend our lives living in, creating, and working with systems. Donella H. Meadows defines a system as "an interconnected set of elements that is coherently organized in a way that achieves something."[8] The society we live in, both local and global, is a system.

Western culture, and the values it has exported across the globe, has been designed to achieve a level of individual and corporate human happiness, flourishing, peace, and prosperity.

Understanding our culture as a system with a function aids us in seeing how it is failing at achieving its goal, delivering bad results that drive our sense of dissatisfaction.

A system contains various parts, which are interconnected. Systems can include:

INPUTS: What is put into the system.

RESERVES: What is stored in the system.

OUTPUTS: What comes out of the system.

CONNECTIONS: The relationships between elements of the system.

An example of a simple system is the rainwater tank in my backyard. It contains an **input**—the rainwater that falls from my roof into the tank. The tank itself is the **reserve**, which can be filled, emptied, or can overflow. The garden hose connected to the tank with which I water my garden is the **output**. The tank is connected to the ecosystem of my garden when I water my plants; I am the **connection**.

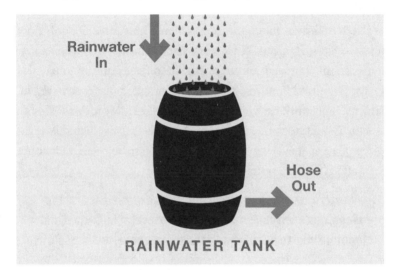

RAINWATER TANK

Now familiar with the basics of a system, we can examine Psalm 1 as a system. The input is God's presence. By delighting in God's presence through His way and His words, health flows into our system. For us as individuals and communities, health will come through God's presence, the revelation of His closeness through His Word, and the wisdom it provides. Most trees are reliant on the vagaries of rainfall, yet here we have a tree by a river, illustrating that God is an ever-present and unwavering input, willing to offer us health and flourishing.

Health flows into our systems through God's presence.

The biblical word for peace in Hebrew is *shalom*. *Shalom* means so much more than merely an absence of war. It also means completeness. "Shalom refers to something that's complex with lots of pieces that's in a state of completeness, wholeness," says Tim Mackie.[9]

God wants to bring shalom to our systems, making them complete, whole, and holy.

Jesus builds on the image of a system filled with shalom. Christ locates this source of fruitfulness in Himself, explicitly telling His followers, "I am the vine; you are the branches. If you remain in me and I in you, you will bear much fruit; apart from me you can do nothing" (John 15:5). Fruit is the result of having God as our input. It's the output that feeds and nourishes others, contributing to the health of a bigger system. For we don't exist as unconnected individuals; we are connected to a more extensive system.

KEY RENEWAL PRINCIPLE
The spiritual fruit that our lives produce is part of God's plan to renew the system we know as the world.

God's Way & Word

Fruit

DESTRUCTIVE INPUTS

Psalm 1 also offers us another illustration, showing us what a toxic and destructive system looks like—a system into which inputs other than God's presence flow. Sin, wickedness, and mockery are used to describe human behaviors and attitudes of the heart that result from choosing to walk away from God's presence in rebellion.

> *Not so the wicked!*
> > *They are like chaff*
> > *that the wind blows away.*
> *Therefore the wicked will not stand in the judgment,*
> > *nor sinners in the assembly of the righteous.*
>
> *For the LORD watches over the way of the righteous,*
> > *but the way of the wicked leads to destruction.*

The person, community, or culture that chooses to "walk in step with the wicked" connects themselves to the input of these ungodly influences, cutting themselves off from the influence of God, and allowing toxicity to flow into their system. The system becomes toxic; the tree no longer flourishes, but dries, dies, becoming "chaff." With such a harmful contagion in its system, the results are devastating. The output is destruction, setting fire to the broader system.

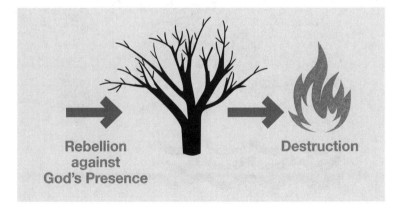

Rebellion against God's Presence → Destruction

WESTERN CULTURE HAS BECOME AN ANTI-RENEWAL SYSTEM

Cultures, individuals, and organizations have only three options—decline, stagnation, or renewal. The growing sense of dissatisfaction about the direction of Western civilization across the board is a signal that our system has become toxic. When we look at Western living standards, levels of peace, prosperity, and development, this can seem a strange outcome. The hardware of the West—our roads, our hospitals, our safety initiatives, our institutions—is good hardware, which creates the possibility of living lives of flourishing. Yet we are running infected software in our system—a vision of individual life, freedom, and happiness that undermines the benefits of our hardware.

> Lifestyles in the West now trend toward immaturity, paralysis, and isolation. At a personal level, the Western life script creates an anti-renewal system. Its inner contradictions and contagions drive us away from flourishing and instead push us into decline.

Of course, some outliers are able to flourish within the West personally—from those who refuse to engage with new technologies, or who possess large reserves of personal will or discipline—yet these people do so by ignoring the powerful formational tools operating across the social and personal environment. Such individuals are definitely the minority, for the system is increasingly rigged against us. To understand this process, let's examine one aspect of the West's inner contradictions to discover how it sets us up to fail. Let's see how this works with our concepts of freedom and individualism.

FREEDOM AT THE EXPENSE OF MEANING

The West is based on a belief that as individuals are given freedom, we will flourish. There is truth in this idea, for it grew at a time in history when most people lived under controlling forms of social, political, and religious control. Humans are happy when we are free, but we also need other things to flourish, such as meaning and deep relational connections. Humans need to know that what we are doing counts, that there is a more significant purpose to our lives, that our decisions and direction matter.

> **We need reserves in our lives of freedom, relationships, and meaning. These reserves need to be balanced with each other, as they are systematically connected in our lives.**

Too much relationality and our individualism may be compromised. The individual who is unable to make any personal choices, to have individual thoughts, or to express a differing opinion, will find that the quality of their life suffers. The West maximizes concepts of freedom. Reacting to the rise of totalitarian regimes like Nazism and Communism in the twentieth century, one of the great fears of the West was the re-emergence of a culture that elevates the rights of the group and enforced codes of meaning upon others at the expense of their individual freedom.

HOW THE LEFT AND RIGHT WORK TOGETHER TO UNDERMINE US

Those on the political right pushed forward with this project of freedom, seeing salvation in the expansion of individual rights, looking to free markets unleashed from government control and restraints. Many on the political left were rightly concerned, seeing this trajectory as creating a kind of mutant hyper-capitalism, mammon on steroids, in which the unbridled pursuit of profit undermined community, relationships, and cultures.

The left was engaged in their own project of expanding freedom, seeing the enemy of freedom in the traditions, structures, and inherited wisdom of the West. Viewing the entire structure of the West as venomously oppressive, they continued their great project of deconstructing preexisting norms such as family, sexuality, gender, language, and culture, the foundational containers in which people found place and meaning. Many on the right were appalled as this project gained pace, seeing little nuance between its approach of rooting out genuine oppression and injustice and what seemed like an indiscriminate carpet bombing of the West's achievements and an endless search to discover or even create new victims and sources of oppression.

In the commotion of the culture war, with eyes fixed on the enemy across the political and cultural divide, what both sides failed to recognize was that for all their differences, they were both working toward the same project.

> **Both the contemporary left and right seek to expand personal freedom as the solution to the human condition.**

The hyper-mutant capitalism and the project of cultural deconstruction work together, pushing the individual into increasing atomization and meaninglessness. Both see the height of human good as the experience of pleasure and positive feelings. Hedonism, the pursuit of pleasure, becomes foundational to our vision of the good life. The individual offered unparalleled consumer choice, the ability to construct an identity, to grasp a bold new future of freedom and opportunity through accelerating technology.

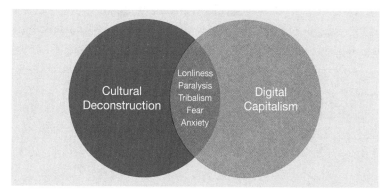

This bold new future ended up looking very different than what we imagined. Instead of the free future that radical individualism promised, our lives became radically reshaped by a combination of technology and consumerism. The very fabric of our habits, thoughts, and behaviors shaped by large corporations and tech giants, who use methods of control that dictators of the past could only dream of.

New technology connects us across time and space, but only in loose ways, offering a tempting alternative to enfleshed forms of human connection. Our new connectivity accelerates the atomization and social isolation already within the system. With cultural forms, traditions, and received wisdom deconstructed, there are few places to find meaning. Hedonism offers countless pleasures but cannot produce meaning.

We are drowning in freedoms but thirsting for meaning.

The individual receives constant messaging from the culture that to be happy and content we need increase our input of freedom. Releasing more freedom into our already overflowing tank of freedom would not solve the problems created in our system by our low reserves of meaning and the relational. Just buying more stuff and consuming more experiences cannot fill these gaps. Our tanks of freedom are overflowing, bursting at the seams, yet our tanks of meaning and the relational are dry and empty.

The output of such a lopsided system is isolation and an increasing mental health crisis of escalating levels of depression and anxiety. The expansion of choice anxiety and information overload has created an endless sense of confusion and lostness, leading many to recoil from making any forward steps, in fear of making the wrong decision. For many, especially in emerging generations, a sense of paralysis has become the norm.

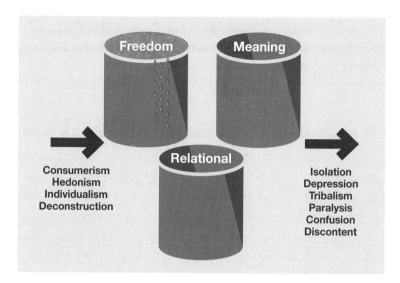

Our Western system is founded on a reading of humans as free individuals who would become happy and content with more freedom.

> **We have forgotten the wisdom that to find happiness and fulfillment, we sometimes need to reduce our freedom to gain meaning and relationships.**

THE RETURN OF TRIBALISM

"When systems do change, they tend to do so relatively rapidly and often quite drastically," notes Joseph O'Connor and Ian McDermott, for "if you put a system under enough pressure for long enough, it can suddenly collapse."[10] With such pressures building up in the Western system, tribalism has returned across our culture both in the identity politics of the left and the return to nationalism on the right. This dynamic only makes our cultural crisis worse, creating constant frictions, outrages, and clashes in our culture, pushing us further into isolation or digital silos of like-minded people.

We become intimately aware of everyone's feelings, concerned about offending someone's shifting emotional landscape. Ambient anxiety accompanies this social dynamic, made worse by constant technological and cultural change.

OUR PERSONAL FAILINGS UNDERMINE OUR CULTURE'S HEALTH

The failing individual system of the West undermines the larger social system of the West, driving the individual toward emotional immaturity and leading the broader culture into decline. The need for renewal becomes acute as the culture begins to regress at an emotional level. Its internal dynamics work against the potential of creating influencers, cultures, and leaders who can lead it out of its descent. As the German philosopher Byung Chul-Han observes, in our emotionally regressing society, "people are turning their aggression against themselves," noting that those who wish for change "are not inclined to revolution so much as depression."[11] So often those who wish for change turn on themselves rather than turning around the communities they are part of. To be effective agents of change, we must understand why this is so.

Chapter 5

Renewal in an Anxious Culture

Fostering Peaceful Presence in the Age of Outrage and Radical Individualism

EMOTIONAL REGRESSION VERSUS RENEWAL

To align ourselves with God's mission of renewal, partnering with Him as He brings healing to the systems of the world, we must understand the emotional landscape of our human systems. This is vital in our highly emotive age, driven by a worship of human feelings.

Systems are highly connected places. Influences, both positive and negative, can spread rapidly within them. Edwin Friedman, a rabbi and family systems theorist, observed the way the toxic anxiety spreads systematically through Western culture, arguing that contemporary culture "has become so chronically anxious that our society has gone into an emotional regression."[1] Despite our foundational belief in progress, the opposite is occurring at an emotional level: "Societal regression is about the perversion of progress."[2] How does this happen? Friedman notes that despite our belief in our radical individualism, we are more connected at emotional levels to each other than we realize, mimicking and drawn into each other's emotions and moods.

We are deeply connected at an emotional level to others.

For Friedman, the chronic anxiety at play in our society is not merely an individual issue but also flows into the social realm: "Chronic anxiety is systemic. . . . Rather than something that resides in the psyche of each one, it is something that can envelop, if not actually connect, people."[3] Anxiety is highly infectious, spreading through the social systems at a swift pace, with the ability to overwhelm us rapidly. Despite our technological advances and the sheer amount of data and information available to us, our emotional landscape shapes our regression.

A feedback loop is at play; our radical individualism and culture of deconstruction have rejected many of the cultural resources—such as community, traditions of moderation and restraint, and even the valuing of routine—with which we historically absorbed social anxiety. With these buffers gone, levels of anxiety escalate. The more anxious the culture became, the more crises were created, leading to poorly thought-through and anxious solutions to our dilemma, exacerbating our problems.

Our Western system has become emotionally feverish.

Friedman saw five characteristics of our emotional regression operating in Western culture:

1) REACTIVITY: The vicious cycle created when individuals and culture continually react intensely to external situations with negative, anxious, angry, and fearful emotions. No longer is the individual or society driven by a set of inner values but instead exists in a state of reactivity, driven by negative external events.

2) *HERDING: Despite our ideology of individualism, our emotional reactivity and our social natures drive us toward others. As the culture becomes reactive, we begin to act in herdlike ways. A mob mentality takes over. The society lowers itself to pleasing and not offending its most emotionally immature and unhealthy members, who then end up dictating the health of the culture.*

3) *BLAME DISPLACEMENT: Instead of examining and searching out the underlying causes creating toxicity, we focus on the symptoms, viewing them in isolation instead of seeing them as part of a systemic whole. Rather than taking a proactive approach that examines our ability to effect change in areas over which we have a responsibility, we retreat into a perpetual victim status, blaming others and external forces. As blame is thrown around, a cultural paralysis sets in. A suffocating fear of offending creates a gridlock, which prevents renewal.*

4) *A QUICK-FIX MENTALITY: Our culture of hedonism has created in us a low pain threshold that prevents us from persevering through the pain that must accompany the processes that lead to breakthrough renewal. Instead, we seek quick-fix solutions, which solve our symptoms rather than the root cause of our crises. We become addicted to technology, more commentary, and more information as the cure for our ills.*

5) *LACK OF WELL-DIFFERENTIATED LEADERSHIP: The above factors create an environment that works against leaders and the kind of leadership that could lead a toxic emotional system into renewal. The influencer must break with the dominant emotional reactivity, toxicity, and blame displacement. Our obsession with the quick fix and low pain threshold ensures that few leaders can push through the isolation of breaking from social herding and reactivity, and the inevitable backlash of the emo-*

tionally regressing environment. No matter how intelligent, tal-ented, or well-equipped leaders may be, ultimately their quest for renewal will be undermined by their own (and the surrounding culture's) low emotional maturity.

A significant challenge then faces us. Our culture—which holds to a myth that it will inevitably progress toward a utopian future, in which individuals also progress morally—is caught in an emotional and moral regression.

The emotionally unhealthy social system entraps potential agents of renewal in its emotional toxicity.

ANXIOUS LEADERS PERPETUATE ANXIOUS SYSTEMS

Friedman discovered that the health of human systems is linked to the leaders in their midst. Whenever he encountered a toxic emotional system in regression, Friedman would inevitably find a leader who had been created by, and who perpetuated, the poisonous system, a leader who was "a highly anxious risk-avoider, someone who is more concerned with good feelings than with progress, someone whose life revolves around the axis of consensus."[4] Consensus can be a good thing, yet in a time of high emotional regression and immaturity, and the resulting fear of offense, consensus ties an organization, family, or church to the will and emotional level of its most immature, dysfunctional, and resistant members, who through consensus are given a lever with which to hold the human system hostage.

Another kind of change agent—the self-differentiated leader— could bring renewal to toxic human systems.

Friedman saw these self-differentiated leaders as being clear about their goals and vision, both at a personal and corporate level, concepts that we are familiar with when it comes to leadership. What made them effective in toxic and emotionally regressing systems was that the self-differentiated leader was someone who was

> *less likely to become lost in the anxious emotional process swirling about. I mean someone who can be separate while still remaining connected and, therefore, can maintain a modifying, non-anxious, and sometimes challenging presence. I mean someone who can manage his or her own reactivity in response to the automatic reactivity of others and, therefore, be able to take stands at the risk of displeasing.*[5]

Internally driven by their goals, vision, and refusal to engage in the environment of ambient anxiety, the self-differentiated leader begins to model a different reality. Their lack of fear begins to inspire others at a profoundly deep and often subconscious level, modeling an alternative to the dominant emotional toxicity. The self-differentiated leader acts like an antibody or a white blood cell, bringing health and renewal into the system.

KEY RENEWAL PRINCIPLE
Live with a peaceful presence in an anxious system, and you will become a healing agent of renewal.

NONANXIOUS LEADERS WILL FACE BACKLASH

The more anxious and dysfunctional members of the human system, however, would sense a threat as the self-differentiated no longer sought their consensus, modeling an alternative way of renewal and health, forcing them to confront the reality that there was a possible path out of their dysfunction. Fearing they had lost their lever of control to bring the system down to their level, the self-differentiated leader becomes a threat. Significant backlash begins, with the self-differentiated leader experiencing undermining, gossip, backstabbing, and emotional reactions.

It is easy to see such undermining as a contemporary phenomenon. One only needs to glance at the pages of church history to see this is not the case. Charles Simeon[6] raised the level of ministry during his lifetime, sponsoring a whole generation of influential ministers, and laying the groundwork for a nationwide renewal in eighteenth-century Britain. However, his desire for reformation resulted in an undermining of his ministry. Simeon endured slanderous attacks from his denominational superiors. So toxic was the state of contemporary culture, the windows in his church were smashed as he preached.[7] Simeon effectively used Bible studies in the homes of those whose lives were being transformed by God, but this was less of a clever innovation than a pragmatic one, as his own church wardens would lock him out of his own church. Those who desire reform will find themselves being resisted.

Through forcing them into isolation, the anxious system seeks to reject the antibody of the nonanxious leader.

NERVE AND COURAGE

Friedman saw this reactivity and undermining as the first sign that the system was turning toward renewal. The emotional toxicity was disturbed by a healthy agent, and thus the process of transformation was beginning. What was essential at this point was for the self-differentiated leader to stay self-differentiated. They must push through the emotional reactivity and backlash. To bring renewal, they had to persist, taking a stand against toxicity, embracing the social isolation that came with being an agent of renewal. Returning to Simeon, we see this dynamic in play as his biographer writes, "It was this total loneliness of his experience which was to influence his personality for the rest of his life. He was driven into an aloneness with

God where . . . he found comfort and encouragement and the power to remain faithful."[8] Simeon came to understand that he was being taught to obey God rather than humans. Eventually, this hidden life with God would become magnetic. A remarkable community of believers would grow around Simeon of those drawn to his life in God. This community would act as a cell of regeneration within the Church of England.

> **If the self-differentiated leader remained as a nonanxious presence, present within the toxic system, eventually their courage would become infectious, and renewal would occur within the social system.**

All that was required was for the self-differentiated leader to hold their nerve in the face of full-scale backlash, reactivity, and rebellion. Something far easier said than done.

Friedman passed away during the publishing of his final book in 1996. His description of a culture in emotional regression has only grown in intensity in our day. The reactivity has reached fever pitch. Social media, smartphones, and wearable technology immerse us in emotional reactivity of such a magnitude that Friedman could never have imagined. News media revolves around emotional reactivity. A handful of tweets from reactive individuals to a particular news item now becomes the basis for entire articles.

OUTRAGE CULTURE

Companies go into public-relations meltdowns when a handful of negative comments are posted on their Facebook page. Colleges, companies, and churches rightly attempt to create warm, welcoming, and inclusive environments, yet can find themselves held hostage by the most emotionally dysfunctional members of their social system. Social media has created a digital megaphone for the venting of negative emotional and toxic reactions that has changed our political and social landscape.

One is left agreeing with Friedman's diagnosis and remedy, but asking, How does one stay self-differentiated? How do we remain nonanxious in a system that continually spirals into new and all-encompassing emotional toxicity? How do we also avoid the potential trap of reacting to our overly sensitive and emotionally entrapped culture by swinging to the opposite extreme of becoming a brute, bashing our way through the social structure, dragging the system toward our own misguided goals? Those wishing to be nonanxious leaders can find themselves in the face of the challenge, descending into a posture that appears nonanxious but is a flawed project of human striving. We can, therefore, appreciate Friedman's illuminating diagnosis and the practical wisdom he brings as to how renewal works in the reality of human systems. A key is missing, the essential component of renewal, what Pete Greig, founder of the 24/7 prayer movement, calls the presence paradigm.[9]

THE PRESENCE PARADIGM

A wise question to ask at this point is how and why self-differentiated and nonanxious leaders create renewals in toxic systems. In his study of human systems, Friedman discovered that what brought healing to emotionally toxic and regressing systems was not the leader's intelligence, nor certain techniques or tactics or even talent, but "what counts is the leader's presence and being."[10] The leader would not even have to engage in constant intimate communication or relationship with individuals in their organization to have a healing effect; "by the very nature of his or her being,"[11] through the physical presence, the leader could release renewal in the system. The most important factor in being an agent of renewal was not "how much power they exercise but how well their *presence* is able to preserve that society's integrity."[12] It wasn't about what they did. It was about who they were. It wasn't about doing. It was about being.

The leader's presence was the paradigm that effected change. It held the key to the renewal of the social system.

Friedman argues that presence is so powerful a change agent because it regulates our emotional responses at a deep and mostly unspoken level. There is a more profound truth beneath what Friedman has identified. For the greatest healing agent in the cosmos is the presence of God. The story of renewal is the story of God's presence returning to our toxic and regressing human lives, systems, and societies.

KEY RENEWAL PRINCIPLE
A revival is when the presence floods a church, a city, or a country, becoming a powerful force that completely reorients the health of that system.

Sin is the root of our anxiety, our toxic emotions, and our systems that trend toward dysfunction. The result of sin is the withdrawal of God's presence. For He is a holy God, the ultimate standard of good, righteousness, and justice. He cannot countenance compromise with sin. Adam's and Eve's decision in the garden to go it alone resulted in the fall of humanity. The result of this fall was a thick and sticky stream of anxiety that runs through human history, oozing into our lived experience. The root of our emotional toxicity, our deep anxiety, and our fears lies in the absence of His presence.

KEY RENEWAL PRINCIPLE
The story of the Bible is the story of the return of His presence. To grasp this truth is to understand the essence of renewal.

YOU CANNOT DO THIS IN YOUR OWN STRENGTH. THIS IS GOOD.

I have tried to live as a nonanxious presence, a self-differentiated leader in the face of constant criticism, undermining, and backlash. Let me tell you, for me this is a continual reality, for Australians have turned attacking and undermining leaders into one of our great national arts. We even have a name for it—the tall poppy syndrome, in which the taller poppies are cut down to size. Despite all of my attempts at discipline, perseverance, humility, and courage, I have learned that I cannot be a nonanxious agent of renewal in my own strength.

I believe that we can only become agents of renewal, we can only get the required distance from toxicity, when we turn not to our inner values and vision, nor the opinion of others, but rather to the presence of God, who wishes to fill and inhabit us—for us to partner with Him as He floods the world with His presence.

KEY RENEWAL PRINCIPLE
We can only be healing presences in systems without turning toxic ourselves when we first become living temples of His presence.

When our being radiates Him, we become a healing presence in the flawed and failing human systems of the world. Renewal then is not achieved through an act of our human courage or nerve. Instead, it is God's great business in the world. He is moving history toward His ends, the filling of creation with His presence. We tend to focus on tasks of renewal through the lens of self, strategizing and dreaming about how we can create a better future. Richard and Henry Blackaby counsel us that *to live a God-centered life, you must focus on God's purposes, not your own plans. Try to see things from God's perspective rather than from your distorted human view. When God starts to do something in the world, He takes the initiative to tell someone what He is doing. Out of His grace, God involves His people in accomplishing His purposes.*[13]

Being an agent of renewal is joining God in what He is doing. If we are to participate in His renewal, we must understand His plan to fill the world with His presence again. So, it is toward that great plan that we next turn.

Chapter 6

Secularism vs. the Presence

From Temples of Exhaustion to Temples of Presence

SECULARISM IS AN ABSENCE OF THE PRESENCE

Secularism is the attempt to create a system for human flourishing in which the presence of God is absent. As we explore the failings of the life system that secularism has created, we also see the damage that such an absence of God's presence creates. Therefore, any renewal of our culture, any healing and reviving of our personal and social systems, must begin with an understanding of God's presence.

The story of Scripture is the high drama of God's presence in the world. Theologian Keven J. Vanhoozer notes that the life of the church is lived "poised between memory and hope."[1]

> Those hungering for renewal live with one hand holding tightly to the memory of how God's presence has returned mightily in the past and the other hand pointing toward the hope found at the end of the age when God's presence again fills the universe.

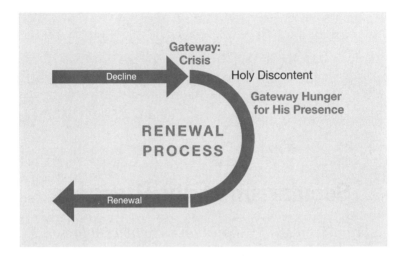

The Bible begins with God's presence filling Eden and ends with the city-temple of New Jerusalem filled with God's presence. God's presence bookends the story of the universe in which we live. To understand this drama and how we are to live within it, wholly fulfilling our roles as agents of renewal, we must examine some familiar elements of Scripture in the fullness of their meaning. Before we can understand the role of God's presence in history and renewal, we must understand the role of those receptacles of God's presence, grasping how temples functioned in the ancient world of the Bible.

TEMPLES AS LIFE SYSTEMS

We think of temples merely as religious buildings, our minds casting back to the role of the temple in the Bible. Temples, however, are an essential clue to how God wishes to renew us.

Temples were at the center of the Gentile nations that surrounded Israel. John Walton writes, "The role of the temple in the ancient world is not primarily a place for people to gather in worship like modern churches. It is a place for the deity—sacred space. It is his home, but more importantly his headquarters—the control room."[2] Idols were housed within these temples, representing the rule of that particular god within the universe. Temples operated as models of the universe. They served as maps of reality, which attempted to mirror the life system of the universe in miniature. They were microcosms—little universes or microworlds.

> Temples operated as models of the life systems of the world. The ideology and religion of a culture illustrated in stone.

As models of the universe, temples operated as control rooms, essential linkages between the divine and human realms. Places that provided a lever of control over reality, where the life system of the universe could be manipulated and pushed toward health, or where neglect could see the cosmos drift again toward chaos. Temples were "considered the center of power, control, and order from which deity brings order to the human world. Fertility, prosperity, peace, and justice emanate from the deity's presence there,"[3] observes Walton, illustrating the importance that the presence of a deity was to the functioning of ancient temples.

TEMPLES GONE WRONG

The pagan gods, seated in their temples, required functionaries who would provide for their needs, satisfying their hunger and thirst through offerings. These gods could become exhausted, thus neglectful of their role in sustaining the life system of the universe, therefore requiring vast amounts of priests and servants to fulfill their hunger. Sometimes through sexual acts performed by worshipers desperate for children or flourishing crops, the gods could be nudged and reminded of their role in providing the power of fertility in the universe.

When the life system of the world seemed to be faltering, the priests and worshipers could cajole and even trick the gods into playing their role through magic and ritual. At their worst, in ancient cultures from the Middle East to South America, in an attempt to manipulate the life system of the universe, temple worship could descend into a bloodbath of human sacrifice.

OUR FAILING TEMPLES OF EXHAUSTION

Understanding that temples are models of our life systems that offer us a chance to move and manipulate our worlds, we can see how our societies, cities, malls, sports stadiums, social media platforms, online habitats, and even our homes operate as temples, microcosms in which, through following the liturgical practices our culture ascribes to us, we try to move the world and our lives toward flourishing.

> Our contemporary culture of progressive secularism is a failing temple, which, like the temples of the ancient world, exhausts and dismays, creating anxious and confused followers.

With hungry gods and impotent idols at the center of their temples, and by extension their life systems, the worshipers of the ancient Gentile world found themselves caught in a descending and dysfunctional codependent relationship with their gods, anxious and exhausting themselves while serving exhaustible gods created by human hands.

Israel's temple also was a model of the universe. God used the forms of the surrounding culture to create a bridge with Israel, but one that was different in radical ways. G. K. Beale writes that "Israel's temples are not like her neighbours merely because they reflected some degree of perception about the true reality of God's dwelling, but because Israel's temple was intended to be viewed as the true temple to which all other imperfect temples aspired."[4]

> Israel's temple was to shine as a prophetic witness, showcasing a flourishing and functioning life system.

Beale contends that Israel's temple was "a protest statement against all other pretenders, of whom she was quite aware. In order to make an effective polemical statement there had to be similarities with the temples of her neighbours, but there also had to be differences."[5] Through understanding these differences, we begin to grasp God's ways of redemption and renewal.

THE FIRST TEMPLE

To understand these vital differences between God-centered temples and the failing temples both ancient and contemporary that place idols at their centers, we must return to the original temple, Eden. In the story of the garden, we find "a creation account focusing on the cosmos as a temple. It is describing the creation of the cosmic temple with all of its functions and with God dwelling in its midst,"[6] writes John Walton. The lynchpin of the cosmos, which makes it a functioning life system, is God's presence, and "without God taking up his dwelling in its midst, the (cosmic) temple does not exist. The most central truth to the creation account is that this world is a place for God's presence."[7] While humans play a role in creation and the life system it creates fulfills our needs, the whole system is centered around Him, "with God's presence serving as the defining element of existence."[8] We can see therefore that any functioning and flourishing temple or life system needs the following elements:

1) THE PRESENCE OF GOD

We can now see that the first difference between Israel's temples and other failing temples and life systems, both ancient and modern, is the presence or absence of God's dwelling. Without God's dwelling within, a temple is not indeed a temple. Just as Solomon's temple became functional when it was filled with God presence, the same temple became dysfunctional when the glory of God departed during the time of Ezekiel. We can also see in Genesis 1 that while the Spirit of God hovered over the unformed chaos of the world, it did not become the world until on the seventh day, having fashioned creation as His temple, God came to dwell. In Genesis, we even find Him casually walking in the garden. Any life system, therefore, needs His presence to flourish and function.

2) IMAGE-BEARERS RATHER THAN IDOLS

The idols at the center of the ancient pagan temples were fashioned out of human hands, therefore representing the image of their makers, including their limitations and failings. In contrast, God creates humans in His image. He gives them a priestly role as His agents in the world. They are to care for His temple of creation. This role points to the crucial next difference between idolatrous temples and God's temples.

3) THE EXPANDING TEMPLE

When Adam and Eve are commanded by God to "be fruitful and increase in number," they are to go beyond Eden, and to "Fill the earth," subduing it. Just as God had subdued and brought order out of the chaos, so the humans will go beyond Eden, spreading the garden by making the places beyond it habitable. Beale writes, "Adam was to widen the boundaries of the Garden in ever increasing circles by extending the order of the garden sanctuary into the inhospitable outer spaces. The outward expansion would include the goal of spreading the glorious presence of God."[9] Humanity's original role and function in God's life system was to act as His agents in the world, expanding His presence through the world, until the whole of creation is filled with His glory. Other temples did not have this capacity to grow; instead, they were merely structures that housed idols, entrapping followers in a claustrophobic cycle of fear and manipulation. At times during the history of Israel, this expansion seemed to be paused, such as when the temple was situated in Jerusalem. Yet with Jesus' death and resurrection, we again see this advancing and expansion of the living temple of His church in the world, until the image of the world as a temple that we glimpse in the book of Revelation.

4) GOD'S TEMPLE SHOWCASED HIS GREATNESS

On the seventh day, God entered His creation-temple to rest. The chaos of the world now conquered, He was able to rest. He is Lord of the world, able to rest because no power, entity, or person could defeat Him. He is the one true God. The Gentile temples contained multiple gods with limited dominions, ruling over fields of human endeavor such as agriculture, or specific regions or cities. In contrast, Yahweh is God of all, unbound by geography, people, or nature. Therefore, where the worship of idols exists, His presence cannot fully dwell, for He is a jealous God. His presence is evidence of His lordship.

5) GOD'S TEMPLE HOLDS TOGETHER HEAVEN AND EARTH

The temple was a place where heaven and earth overlapped. Tom Wright writes that temples "hold together the divine realm ('heaven') and the human realm ('earth')."[10] They were places where both God and humanity communed, where God was truly present, and humans—holy, obedient, and in relationship with their Father—were also truly present as human beings.

FROM PRESENCE TO ABSENCE

Adam and Eve's mission to operate as agents of God's presence as it spreads across the world was dependent on their obedience. They were to follow God's Torah—His instructions—and His first instruction to Adam and Eve was that they were to be nourished by any food in the garden except the tree of the knowledge of good and evil. The role of a priest was also to protect the sanctity of the temple from things that are unclean. The appearance of the serpent in the garden hints at a dereliction of priestly duties that was possibly already in play before the snake asked his dangerous question.

> ## The temple was the arena in which priests partnered with God to ensure that the world flourished.

The expansion of God's presence was to progress at God's pace, as Adam and Eve spread out and brought His glory across the face of the world. The endpoint of history we read of in the book of Revelation, according to Beale, presents "the entire new heavens and earth to be one mammoth temple in which God dwells."[11] Hence history was heading toward God's perfect end and unfolding according to His plan. The serpent offered another vision of progress, which appealed to something that was brewing inside the first couple. Peter Leithart notes that

> *Adam and Eve were created as flesh—limited, weak, vulnerable, touchable, woundable. That was good, very good. They might have accepted their vulnerability and the precariousness of their fleshly life, trusting the Father to care for them. Adam might have been content to wait for the Lord to open his hand to satisfy his desires, might have trusted his Father to give him his full inheritance when the Father saw that he was ready. Eve might have rejoiced in fleshly weakness and trusted her Father to supply whatever strength she needed. Instead, they were discontented and impatient. Created good, very good flesh, they wanted to be more, and they wanted to be something more now.*[12]

Through a combination of negligence, disobedience, impatience, and discontent with God's rule, lack of trust, and rebellion, Adam and Eve choose their human-powered vision of progress. They risk it all in a quest to discover a divine presence within themselves. Cast out of God's presence, they find nothing, only the taste of bitter fruit.

Priests were to guard the holy spaces against those who were unclean; now Adam and Eve themselves are unclean, unable to enter the sacred space of Eden, the dwelling place of the presence.

> In choosing their autonomy apart from God, Adam and Eve rejected their priestly role.

A VOCATION AND A MISSION REJECTED

Expelled from Eden, Adam and Eve lose their divinely given roles. Their mission reversed in curses.[13] They were to till the soil, expanding the garden; now, however, the earth is hardened and cursed, slowing this expansion. They were to be fruitful and multiply, through their offspring spreading His presence across the world. Now childbearing will be difficult and painful. Most appallingly, Adam and Eve are no longer agents of His presence.

> Their constant companion was no longer God's presence, but instead shame, anxiety, and isolation.

PROGRESS WITHOUT PRESENCE

The expulsion of Adam and Eve from the garden is at first glance an extreme measure. However, such divine measures are essential, for they operate as needed restraints on Adam and Eve, who now have chosen to be agents of chaos, trying to pursue expansion and dominion without God. They desire progress without presence. Such a dangerous project must be hindered by God, for it threatens to ruin the world. Adam and Eve swap their human flesh, which lives under the protection of God in His presence, for flesh disconnected from God's presence, now mortal and frail. They inhabit flesh transformed, symbolic of humanity's weakness but also their rebellion against God and desire for self-sufficiency.

> Human flesh, cut off from the presence, mutates into
> something monstrous—a force that resists the expansion
> of God's presence out into the world.

God's image-bearers still do procreate and expand out into the world in their strength. As Ryan Lister reminds us, "Adam, the one created to be God's priest and king is without a kingdom and without a temple."[14] Adam and Eve's offspring will thus go out across the world and history with eternity still written on their hearts—the divine imprints of priesthood and worship, a longing for a home in the presence of God that they cannot name—and create temples and life systems inhabited not by God but by idols.

GOD REFUSES TO ABANDON HIS CHILDREN

Such a devastating and destructive outcome could seem to be the end of the story. God does not give up on His plan to fill the earth with His presence. Despite their rebellion and rejection of life in His presence, God would not abandon His children. He would still seek them out. To protect humans from the death that would occur if they entered the fullness of His presence in their unclean state of fallenness and fleshly rebellion, His presence now would now have to be mediated and partial.

> His presence would be mediated through fire, cloud,
> sacrifice, temples, curtains, and codes of purity.
> There could be a relationship, but only mediated through
> religion. There still could not be full life in His presence.
> The relationship remained fractured.

A BUILDING CRESCENDO CRYING OUT FOR GOD'S PRESENCE

There is not time or space here to explore this history fully. The story of the Old Testament—from the story of God sacrificing animals for their skins to cover Adam and Eve's shame, His appearance to Moses in a burning bush and on a mountain, His dwelling in the holiest of holies in the tabernacle and temple, to the cries of prophets both major and minor for His return—this is the story of God's plan to flood the world with His presence. It is also the story of saints, prophets, and kings, a building crescendo of contending prayer, crying out for the return of His presence, a remnant that could not tolerate any longer the failed reign of human flesh, that longed for God's holy rule and dominion.

These prayers culminated in Simeon, hungering for the return of God's presence, moved by the Spirit to head to the temple. Also the elderly prophetess Anna, robbed of her husband early in her marriage, waiting and yearning for God to come, barely leaving the temple, fasting and praying day and night. It is Simeon's and Anna's hands that touch the baby in the temple who will be the sacrifice, whose death will tear the curtain in the temple, allowing His presence to again flood into the world. It is to this baby, this man, this God, to whom we next turn.

KEY RENEWAL PRINCIPLE
Every renewal, every revival, is about Jesus.

Chapter 7

Renewal to the Ends of the Earth

God's Plan to Fill the Cosmos with His Presence

RELEASING THE PAUSE BUTTON

The word *renew* means to continue something after it is paused. This is what happens to God's plan to fill the world with His presence through His children. They again renew, re-engaging their calling to partner with God in the spreading of His presence in the world. To renew is also to bring fresh life to something that is exhausted or degenerate. The story of the Bible after the disobedience of humans is one of renewal.

> ### KEY RENEWAL PRINCIPLE
> **God's whole business is renewal. When we engage in it, we follow His ways.**

God had not given up on His plan to fill the world with His presence; He draws near to Abraham, reinstituting the command to go into the world to flourish and be fruitful. He draws near to Israel, beginning the process of shaping them into a people among whom He can dwell. The temptation faced by Adam and Eve will also be ever-present for Israel. The opportunity to pursue freedom and to flourish under the steam of their power will continue the trend of disobedience amongst God's people.

THE WAY OF OBEDIENCE

Israel will discover that there are two alternatives to renewal. First, in an attempt to preserve their own will and human strength, they may choose to resist God's renewal, their flesh, in disobedience, forming a blockade against the entry of God's presence. The second option is to attempt to engage in renewal in their strength, to join in renewal without God's presence. Both options actively work against God's plan to fill the world with His presence.

KEY RENEWAL PRINCIPLE
The path to renewal is paved with obedience.

God had come close to Israel, yet His people still lived under the flesh. "Salvation would mean the reversal of this fallen condition," writes Peter Leithart. "Salvation would bring free admission to eat and drink in God's presence. Salvation would involve deliverance from mortal flesh, and from the taboos and exclusions that resulted from it. Anyone who could achieve that would be the Savior of Adam's race."[1]

God's plan would still involve the end goal of filling the world with His presence and glory. It also must deal with the eradication of flesh and disobedience. Thus, in His coming to earth, in His incarnation, we see several key elements of God's presence.

1) GOD'S PRESENCE IS THE GOAL OF HISTORY. God's presence is directed to the end of the age, to the New Jerusalem, for His presence will fill the earth.

2) GOD'S PRESENCE IS HIS MEANS OF ACCOMPLISHING THIS GOAL. While history will end with God's presence, throughout human history, He uses His presence as the means of achieving this goal.

3) GOD'S PRESENCE IS LOVE. It shows His desire to draw near to His people and to dwell amongst them as He did in Eden and will in the New Jerusalem. We were created to be in relationship with Him.

4) GOD'S PRESENCE IS JUSTICE. His presence comes to wage war against that which resists His goal of filling the world with His glory. His presence is also His justice. It comes to remove from the world unredeemed flesh, disobedience, injustice. It comes to destroy our attempts to pursue our original Adamic vocation in our strength.

All of these threads would tie into a knot in the life of Jesus. He will be called Immanuel—God with us—to fulfill the promise that God will be with His people. Ryan Lister notes, "Christ's being Immanuel is a gateway to the promises of God and his redemptive purposes. The presence of God once enjoyed in a measure by the patriarchs and by Moses and Israel at Sinai is now manifest in the person of Jesus Christ. And like the presence of Yahweh in the Old Testament, Christ comes to his people to work salvation and restore to them the covenant blessings."[2]

Jesus is therefore not just God's presence amongst us. He is God's redemptive presence, sent to renew us, to complete God's goal of moving history toward His full presence.

He shows us the end of history, but also how we are going to get there. Lister continues, "Being the fulfillment of the Immanuel sign and all its implications reveals that Christ is the completion of God's Old Testament promise to be with His people for their redemption, while simultaneously working to consummate God's promise to re-open access to God's . . . presence."[3]

His early years show Him shaped in the ways of God in the temple, learning and following, dwelling in the house of the Lord. His ministry begins with baptism and the empowering of the Spirit for ministry. He announces through His preaching that the kingdom was here. God had drawn near. Despite opposition, the crowds, the stubbornness and difficulty of His disciples, He continually retreats to spend time with His Father.

> **Jesus models the perfect life system—at the center is abiding with the Father. His life is an act of total worship and service to God.**

Unlike Adam, Jesus' life is marked by obedience. He shows us how the Spirit of God can exist in a person and be spread by the Spirit by living in the Spirit. He is the presence enfleshed.

KEY RENEWAL PRINCIPLE
Jesus is a walking renewal.

As we have learned, the presence is not just the destination but also the road to get there. We see in Jesus this dynamic at work; for those of contrite, meek, and humble hearts, Jesus' presence comes as a balm. Living water to fill dehydrated souls. The poor of Israel, who according to earthly metrics had nothing, have little to lose and everything to gain as the presence walks amongst them. For the rich and the proud, however, the willful and resistant, the same presence stings.

THE PRESENCE WAGES WAR ON THE FLESH

Jesus comes to wage war on the flesh, and indeed the forces of flesh, the demons, those who wish not to lay down their lives. To the elements of the religious establishment that have calcified into religiosity without presence, to the Roman machine built on fleshly power, the presence of God come near must be destroyed.

> This dynamic shows us that the presence will divide— recognized by those who hunger after God as pure love, seen by forces controlled by the flesh as a threat to be resisted.

Jesus was changing the spiritual superstructure of the world, telling those who would listen that soon He must die. Peter Leithart writes,

> *After Adam's expulsion from the garden, holy space became taboo, inaccessible space. Yahweh stationed cherubim at the gate of the garden to guard against every attempt at reentry. From Adam on, if anyone wanted to enter the presence of God, he would have to pass through the sword and fire of the cherubim. No man could return to feast in the presence of God unless he first died.*[4]

Jesus would die, to again open up access to the presence.

Adam's and Eve's disobedience in the garden had reversed their mandate to fill the world with God's presence, instead filling it with flesh, disobedience, death, and sin. On the cross, Jesus' death defeats these blockages to God's renewal of the world. His death, the final sacrifice, means those who follow Him no longer must approach the presence through mediated forms of temple worship and sacrifice.

The presence gives His life upon the cross so that humans may again enter His presence.

INCARNATION

Jesus' driving of the sellers out of the temple is a critique not just of the Jerusalem temple, but of all temples, all life systems, all concepts of worship, that operate not with God's presence but with human flesh, sin, and striving at their core. Jesus had spoken of the temple being torn down and raised after three days. To those around Jesus with their flesh-encased minds, such a prediction seemed preposterous. Jesus, however, was speaking of a deeper reality. He had become the new temple, containing the presence of God, fulfilling the sacrifices that will allow the people of God to enter into His presence.

> All other temples fell short, all other competing life systems were defeated upon the cross—they would go on, but their game was up.

For the spirit of all renewals is the Spirit of Jesus. In every true renewal, both individual and corporate, Jesus is lifted up. He is central. He inspires and animates growth, healing, and regeneration. As the new temple Himself, He is on a mission to renew our temples, our sites of worship, our life systems. We need to grasp this concept clearly as we cry out for renewal.

Jesus on the cross becomes the final sacrifice. As He dies, the curtain in the temple, the mediating veil, which protects unclean humans from the pure glory of God's presence, is torn from top to bottom. With the final sacrifice now fulfilled upon the cross, God Himself removes the barrier that He had placed at the gates of Eden. Until this point, the temple was to operate with magnetic power, drawing the seekers after God's presence to Him. Sin and striving had prevented this. Now, however, the situation was reversed; the Jerusalem temple would shortly fall, destroyed by the hordes of Rome.

Jesus, the new temple, was to birth a new kind of people of
God, a new temple, built not of stone, but ordinary human lives,
drawn together, transformed and filled with His presence.

ASCENSION

Following His resurrection, Jesus ascends as to the right hand of the
Father, going ahead into the full presence of God found in the heavenly court. By ascending, Jesus appears to leave.

This departure initially seems to run against the grain of God's
plan to fill the world with His presence. But as Anthony J. Kelly
writes, this leaving, this ascension, is key to His plan to fill the world
with His glory:

> *He is then taken up into the luminous cloud of God's presence, no
> longer to be found in the time and space of his early life in Palestine. . . .
> In his ascended existence, he now fills all time and space, and inhabits
> every dimension of reality, from the highest realm of the infinite
> Godhead to the mundane, agonizing reality of created existence.
> This ascension opens the space in which believers themselves begin to
> inhabit a new sphere of transformed existence.*[5]

By leaving, Jesus comes back in a new way. For now, "the whole
of creation is filled with Christ's saving presence. From the glory of
heaven, Christ fills the space left by His earthly absence. He has
opened our world to the hitherto impenetrable reality of heaven."[6]
Jesus has gone ahead into the full glory of God. On earth, He showed
the way to be fully human and wholly obedient to God.

Now, ascended, Christ goes ahead, living and directing the
world, dwelling in the unmediated presence of God.

As the writer of Hebrews states, in this new arrangement, "We have
confidence to enter the Most Holy Place by the blood of Jesus, by a new

and living way opened for us through the curtain, that is, his body, and since we have a great priest over the house of God, let us draw near to God" (Heb. 10:19–22). A new era had broken out in human history. Jesus, living in the fullness of His presence. And through us, that future breaking into the world, playing out in real time.

This new era took some getting used to. Moments after Jesus' ascension, the disciples, bemused and staring at the sky, are reoriented by the angels, who question their intense vertical gaze. With Jesus now ascended, God's plan to fill the cosmos with His presence continues with a new intensity and power. The disciples' gaze must now be horizontal, out into the world, their posture to be an active one; reconnected with the original mandate given to Adam and Eve, they are to go out into the world.

SPIRIT

One can imagine how His disciples would have felt that after dying on the cross and having been raised from the dead after three days, Jesus' presence would become essential to their moving forward with the mission to spread God's glory into the world. After His ascension, as Andrew Murray writes, the disciples "never for a moment regretted His bodily absence; they had Him with them, and in them, in the divine power of the Holy Spirit."[7] Jesus taught them that He had to go for the Spirit to come. This was the plan.

> The church, empowered by the Holy Spirit, now takes
> His presence across the world.

Adam was to partner with God in the spreading of His presence across the world through instructing his offspring in the ways of God and sending them out. Jesus, as the new Adam, achieves what the first Adam could not. After His resurrection, Jesus instructs His disciples about the kingdom of God. They are then to be sent out into creation to spread the presence. Unlike Adam, they are not to go out in their power, cut off from the presence of God. Instead, they are to wait until the power of the presence comes upon them in the form of the Spirit.

> *"You will receive power when the Holy Spirit comes on you; and you will be my witnesses in Jerusalem, and in all Judea and Samaria, and to the ends of the earth." (Acts 1:8)*

The disciples are sent out from Jerusalem, God's temple city. In a few short years, the temple in Jerusalem will fall, just as Jesus predicted, destroyed by the Romans. Now the people of God will become a living temple, filled with the presence, each of them a mini-temple, filled with His Spirit, who through living in His presence, spread His presence throughout the world. We see Paul exhorting the church in Corinth, passionately reminding them that they "are God's temple and that God's Spirit dwells in [their] midst" (1 Cor. 3:16). Peter describes the church as human stones (1 Peter 2:5), a new kind of temple not constructed with stone but with human lives, which are being built into a "spiritual house." Reading these Scriptures, we begin to grasp that humans are only truly human in the presence, finding meaning and purpose only when they align their desires, hopes, and lives with His plan.

The human life is only a functioning life system when we live as temples filled with the presence.

But as Jesus taught, this kind of life is a narrow path, and the way to destruction is spacious and smooth. The indwelling of sin in the world would mean that this epoch—the time between Jesus' death, resurrection, and ascension, the coming of the Spirit and the sending of the church and His eventual return at the end of the age—would be one in which the energy of renewal would continually need to be released.

KEY RENEWAL PRINCIPLE
The church, filled with God's Spirit, acts as His renewing
agent in the life system of the world.

THE PRESENCE INJECTED INTO THE VEINS OF THE EMPIRE

The presence would now go out. Spread by this new living temple, the church—a dwelling place of the presence. It would flow into the bloodstream of the Roman system of human power, bringing life and health. The mission of spreading the presence would use the very structures of roads, sea lanes, cities, and infrastructure built to facilitate the expansion of human power and striving, repurposing them, spreading the gospel and God's presence across land masses and continents to the ends of the earth. Those very communities and churches built around the presence, like Israel, would find themselves engaged in a debilitating process. Slowly, the presence would be less central to the life of the church, as the temptation to again trust in human rather than divine power would see the very structure created to house the presence instead become a stronghold of the flesh again.

Chapter 8

Why the Church Needs Renewal

Embracing Hot Orthodoxy and Vital Christianity

WHEN THE FIRE COOLS

Having now explored God's plan to renew the world through His bride, the church, filled with His Spirit, we must ask a question that is difficult yet essential for understanding the dynamic of renewal. Why do we see such a gap between the power and presence of God that we read of in the early church and our contemporary experiences of church and faith? How do churches and individuals, renewed by the Spirit and presence of God, find themselves falling into decline and stagnation? To understand this, we must return to the early church.

The apostles, renewed by the power of the Spirit, engage with God's purpose to fill creation with His presence, go out into the world and multiply. Across the Greco-Roman world, the church and the presence spread, as believers are born and find access to the Father through Jesus, the new High Priest. In the letters of the early church that now make up part of our New Testament, the story is not one of unfaltering growth.

Within decades of the fire experienced at Pentecost, a cooling occurred amongst the people of God.

Christ rebukes the church in Laodicea in the book of Revelation for a faith that is neither hot nor cold, but lukewarm.

WHY DOES THE CHURCH NOT CONTINUALLY ADVANCE?

Reflecting on these dynamics, we ask with Richard Lovelace, if Jesus has come, and a new spiritual era has broken out in human history, "Why is the advance of the Christian church not continuous? Why is it subject to periods of decline and recovery which so closely resemble the cyclical pattern of the Old Testament?"[1] We see the elements mentioned above seemingly causing a reversal of the gains of the gospel.

Howard A. Snyder argues that there is evidence of a renewal movement within a generation of the early church, indicating "both the decline of spiritual vitality in the church and the faith's inherent tendency and push toward new life and fresh energies."[2] We see littered throughout the history of the church both declines and renewals. Sadly, the presence-filled life of the church, and dynamic transformation promised by the potential of the gospel and faith-filled life, is radiant but rare.

FALLING BACK INTO RELIGIOSITY

In his letter to the Galatians, Paul exposes two errors that the church was falling into, both affecting the momentum, growth, and health of the early church. Firstly, there is a return to kinds of religious behaviors that characterized the period in which God's presence must be mediated through temple, ritual, and purity. He calls this a fall back into the elementary principles, a return to an enclosed temple, in which God's presence has not gone out into the world, but stays sealed in a holy space. The church engaging in the sin of the Pharisees that Jesus warned of. A fall back into religiosity—the temptation to return to the fleshly pursuit of making ourselves right with God by our strength. Grace replaced by judgmentalism. Freedom by fear. Mission with suspicion, and holiness with a holier-than-thou facade. Faith is thrown back into a pre-Christian posture, back into the flesh. Even after Christ has come, the failings of Israel can be repeated by those who, like Lot's wife, look backward.

RUNNING AHEAD INTO IRRELIGIOSITY

Secondly, Paul also warns about an opposite error, in which the freedom of the gospel leads to excess, pushing beyond the bounds of what God is advancing into irreligiosity. The freedom of the gospel is twisted into liberty to sin.

> An impatience with God's way and timetable leads to heresy. The temptation is to run ahead of what the Spirit is doing. This is a post-Christian posture that we see even in the early church.

It's an attempt to achieve the mission of the Spirit and step into the freedom that is beyond the guardrails God has erected. Ironically, this flight from limits ends up leading to the same place that the fall back into religiosity does—an imprisoning in the flesh as humans, instead of God, again set the agenda for renewal.

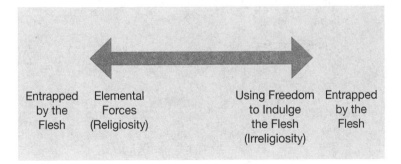

| Entrapped by the Flesh | Elemental Forces (Religiosity) | Using Freedom to Indulge the Flesh (Irreligiosity) | Entrapped by the Flesh |

Before we can explore the dynamics of renewal, we must first understand how the movement of the living presence known as the church finds itself falling into stagnation and decline. We will utilize a number of key terms, outlined below.

KEY TERMS

DEAD ORTHODOXY: When true biblical faith is affirmed with our words and thoughts, but the heart remains stagnant and unchanged. Doctrine is biblical, but the spiritual life of the church or the believer is dead.

COLD ORTHODOXY: Correct biblical faith and doctrine are held. However, a church caught in cold orthodoxy works from the memory of a past move of God. Little vitality exists in the daily spiritual life of the church.

CULTURAL CHRISTIANITY: When Christianity is inherited and affirmed as a cultural identity rather than a lived personal faith. Certain Christian practices are enacted in order to maintain a cultural identity. There may be personal elements of faith, but the dominant framework of Christian practice is held in place by cultural expectations and tradition. The values of a culture mix with faith, blurring lines between both.

VITAL CHRISTIANITY: Correct biblical faith and doctrine is affirmed, alongside a healthy spiritual life of a significant amount of a congregation.

HOT ORTHODOXY: Correct biblical faith and doctrine flow out of a vibrant spiritual life. God moves powerfully. Truth and presence are ever-present. A majority of the congregation lives a powerful and vibrant spiritual life.

DEAD ORTHODOXY

As we have discovered, God's plan to fill the world with His presence through His living priesthood of humans, who have given their lives over to becoming temples filled with His Spirit and moving out into the world, creates a vital church. The vital church centers itself on God's Word, His revelation given to us. The Spirit is present amongst them, guiding them, empowering them, and leading them. They move forward with the purpose of the filling the world with His presence.

The vital church then holds together Spirit, Word, and World (not the common biblical understanding of world as the forces that oppose God, but rather, the human cultures of the world), and as Stuart Piggin notes, "When these three are synthesised the movement is strong and when they are separated the movement is weak."[3]

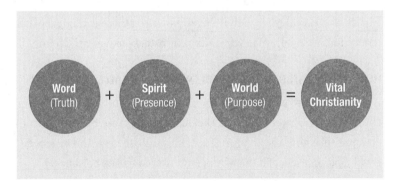

Richard F. Lovelace recounts, "Thus far in time vital Christianity has been a thin stream that sometimes goes underground, only to emerge again to spread abroad like a river that has been dammed, expanding during awakenings to form a reservoir that refreshes and transforms a culture for a generation."[4] What is it that makes this vital Christianity so rare among the annals of Christian history?

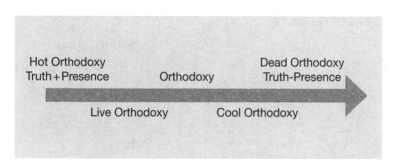

THE DYNAMICS OF DECLINE

To understand dead orthodoxy, we have to understand the temptation to push forward with our purpose in God while neglecting His presence, through a gradual forgetting that typically occurs over generations. *Orthodoxy* is the technical word for believing the right things about God, having a high view of Scripture, correct theology and doctrine. But as we will discover, assenting to a theological list of tenets does not guarantee vital faith nor insulate us against decline.

HOW VITAL CHRISTIANITY DECLINES INTO DEAD ORTHODOXY

A generation encounters truth and power, Word and presence. A vital church emerges out of decline. The people of God are filled with truth and presence, thus they can engage their purpose to go and be spreaders of God's presence in the world, empowered by His presence.

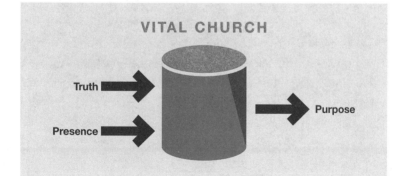

Often the next generation is pushed along by the sheer spiritual momentum of the previous generation that has stepped into His presence and vital faith. Practices, traditions, and institutions are initiated to keep the momentum going and to educate the coming generations on how to maintain the vitality. Yet a temptation can enter at this point to rely on these tools without the total reliance upon the presence. This happens at such a subtle level it can be barely perceptible. Two slow but disastrous changes then occur:

1) WE FILL THE TANK WITH OUR OWN PRIDE AND FLESH

Our desire for independence and autonomy from God, to achieve our God-given purpose under our own steam, to achieve for our own glory. Our quest for personal glory in a raw grab for pride, or the inverted pride of insecurity, leads us to seek recognition and affirmation from humans rather than God. This creates fleshly strongholds of resistance against the presence. We start to get in the way, becoming the primary blockage to Him flooding our life system with His presence. Our capacity for His presence is reduced, because our tank is increasingly filled with our own flesh.

2) WE SLOWLY TURN OFF THE INPUT OF HIS PRESENCE

Striving in our strength to get His work done soon becomes living too busy to engage with His presence. We are not doing bad stuff—in fact, great stuff, more ministry, more programs, more education, more mission, more justice, more social media promotion of His work. Yet soon, chasing our God-given purposes without the power of His presence, our churches, our services, and our lives are packed full. Those empty spaces, in which we wait on Him, His leadings, and His voice disappear. We lose the capacity for voice recognition because we have fully and unquestionably given over to the high-achievement performance lifestyle of the twenty-first-century

West. We may still be theologically orthodox but running on empty, like the church that rightly holds to its orthodox theological creeds but is slowly drained of spiritual vitality, or the believer who mentally assents to correct biblical belief but whose heart is not transformed.

Even those who grasp the intellectual heights of faith can in a moment experience God break through in a profoundly personal and transformative way. After writing possibly the greatest systematic theology in the history of the church, the medieval theologian Thomas Aquinas encountered God in such a profound way while taking communion that he remarked to his friend that compared to what he had seen, his writing was mere straw.[5]

John Wesley, returning to the United Kingdom as a failed evangelical missionary to North America, possessed a keen theological mind, yet was filled with anxiety. His life was radically changed during a service at Aldersgate Chapel, as his "heart was strangely warmed."[6] The brilliant Christian mathematician and scientist Blaise Pascal was intellectually a Christian, yet experienced a profound deepening of his faith, of which he told no one. That was until after his death, his housekeeper found sewed into the lining of his jacket an entry from his personal journal, which attempted to described the immensity of this moment of spiritual insight, dating the entry at around sometime between 10:30 p.m. and 12:30 p.m. Pascal wrote:

Fire
'God of Abraham, God of Isaac, God of Jacob,' not of philosophers and scholars.
Certainty, certainty, heartfelt, joy, peace.[7]

Aquinas, Wesley, and Pascal all discovered that Christianity is more than simply right belief. Right belief is key, but it is ultimately a faith of dynamic personal relationship with the Creator of the universe.

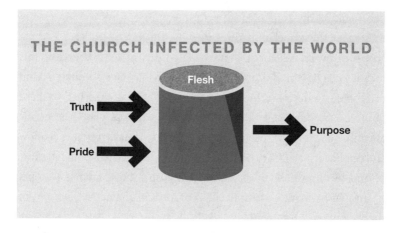

TRENDING INTO DEFEAT

Incrementally, hot orthodoxy, which is alive and vital with the Spirit, cools into cold orthodoxy and eventually calcifies into dead orthodoxy. Everyone believes the right things, assenting to correct doctrine. They have the right information but not the transformation. When we do the right things without the presence, exhaustion will soon appear. Exhaustion then leads to malaise, the gap growing between what is read of in Scripture and the great stories of vitality in church history, and what is experienced in the dead orthodoxy of today.

A kind of theology and ministry practice of reduced expectations kicks in, a gnawing sense of worry sets in with the rise of secularism. Dead orthodoxy doesn't just affect churches; it can be lived by individuals, in which the gap between belief and practice becomes vast.

Dead orthodoxy gives birth to a Christian posture of defeat.

DEAD ORTHODOXY DIMINISHES THE POWER OF THE MESSAGE

Most churches that have fallen into dead orthodoxy are filled with nice, pleasant, and loyal people. Some even grow in size. Yet, eventually the degenerating dynamic of dead orthodoxy diminishes the power and message of the gospel, mutating into what Dallas Willard has called the gospel of sin management. Willard noted that in some churches, this meant behavior modification, avoiding obvious sins through a kind of religious willpower. In other more left-leaning churches, Willard observed another kind of behavior modification at play—the public affirming of the right social justice causes of the day. Yet these shallow and public forms of Christianized behavior management both fall short of transforming vital faith: "The current gospel then becomes a 'gospel of sin management.' Transformation of life and character is no part of the redemptive message," lamented Willard.[8]

For people in dead orthodoxy, Richard Lovelace writes that "their understanding of sin focuses upon behavioral externals which they can eliminate from their lives by a little will power and ignores the great submerged continents of pride, covetousness and hostility beneath the surface." The surface may appear presentable, but underneath, the flesh still reigns; thus such people may seem to be good Christian folk, leading reputable lives, visibly advocating for causes of justice, volunteering, and even leading, yet underneath lies not the presence, but a humanly powered engine. Such people, while appearing as functional and even faithful believers, unwittingly work against the flourishing of the vital church. "Their pharisaism defends them both against full involvement in the church's mission and against full subjection of their inner lives to the authority of Christ."[9] Their agreement with the tenets of good biblical faith masks that one of their feet is in the camp of the Pharisees.

Dead orthodoxy creates Pharisees.

The Pharisees were a significant reform movement within Judaism, advocating for a return to biblical faith. In much they were in agreement with Jesus, yet their patterns of renewal could not change the human heart. As Jesus showed, hypocrisy undergirded their surface-level religious observance. Jesus uses the Pharisees as an example to teach us that hypocrisy will inevitably accompany dead orthodoxy. This can exist at a personal level, in which the right beliefs are affirmed, but in the private spaces sin operates the levers of the control room. It can also exist at a corporate level, in which orthodox faith statements are held, affirmed, and preached, yet hypocritical views and actions are pursued that blatantly contradict biblical faith.

This can range from attitudes of judgmentalism, criticism, and division, but also can trend into truly disturbing territory. One only has to think of the historical record—the complicity of German Lutherans in Nazism, Reformed Christians in South African apartheid, American Southern Baptists in lynching, Northern Irish evangelicals in sectarianism, and Rwandan Pentecostals in tribal genocide.

CULTURAL CHRISTIANITY

Dead orthodoxy does not always lead to such horrifying conclusions, but rather the stagnation or decline that occurs with cultural Christianity, where faith is simply something passed on with a cultural identity—the American evangelical, the English Anglican, or the Croatian Catholic.

> Nothing is more beautiful than a culture or nation baptized in the way of the kingdom, yet nothing is uglier than when faith is confused with the power claims of a culture or nation.

Cultural Christianity then moves into the toxic territory beyond dead orthodoxy, exacerbating hypocrisies, and the distance between the universal plan of God to fill the world with His presence and cultural forms of Christianity grows.

CRISES LEAD TO HOLY DISCONTENT

Inevitably such hypocrisy leads to a crisis. Either the movement or church dies, or the crisis of the corruption of cultural Christianity kicks in. The gap between what is taught and lived leads to dissatisfaction.

> Dissatisfaction has the potential to ferment into a holy discontent.

First, this holy discontent grabs an individual. Then a handful. Soon, a minority, who in their holy discontent goes searching and reconnects with the vision of a vital Christian faith, inspired by Scripture, the Spirit, and the great models of renewal and the vital Christianity of the past. This remnant gains momentum, growing into a renewing impulse, throwing themselves back onto the mercy of God. The flesh is fought and expelled. People cry out again to God, at the end of themselves and realizing their helplessness without heaven's help.

> **KEY RENEWAL PRINCIPLE**
>
> **In renewal, the great beliefs of Christianity no longer are seen as just timeless truths but lived realities.**

Lived realities that transform hearts, churches, and communities. A new release of vital Christianity into individuals' lives and churches. "Believers break through complex, abstract, obscure theology and get to the basic practical truth of the Scriptures," observes Lewis Drummond, noting that this does not mean that renewal creates an anti-intellectual climate but instead "an empirical, purely rationalistic theology that downgrades the transcendental elements of Christianity are laid to rest in awakenings. People become vividly alive to the fact that the sovereign miracle-working God is among them."[10] This may happen on a small or large scale. Lives, churches, movements, and communities are reformed and rebuilt after previous collapses and crises. A new world of solidity and vitality grows into being. Formation and presence are still held alongside each other in a fruitful, creative tension. While this continues, renewal and new life will be normative.

RUNNING INTO IRRELIGIOSITY

Renewal can also run into toxic territory when it falls into the other temptation that Paul warned about—losing itself in the freedom that comes with the gospel and indulging in the flesh. The same renewal process occurs in the description above, but instead of falling back into dead orthodoxy and cultural Christianity, the renewal energy hurtles forward beyond the boundaries of orthodox faith. The historic tenets are jettisoned, Scripture ignored, in place of the sacred scripture of contemporary Western programs of social renewal.

The enemy, content when Christians stay frozen in stagnation, will do everything he can not to wake the believers, lest they again realize their true purpose as carriers of the presence.

> However, when holy discontent turns into a renewing impulse, like a judo master, Satan's effective tactic is to throw that energy beyond a move of God, running ahead of His presence.

Hurtling out beyond orthodoxy and into a humanly driven project of renewal will inevitably trend first into heresy and then lead into decline. A diminishing of the Word occurs, and the voice of the Spirit is confused with the spirit of the age. Worldliness takes over, secular renewal energies are mistaken for moves of God.

It is a sobering thought that North Korean dictator Kim Jong Un's grandfather Kim Il-sung was born into a devout Presbyterian family, which was part of the generation of Koreans touched by the revival that broke out on the peninsula. As their country suffered invasion and poverty, young Christians began to infuse their faith with the secular renewal energy of Marxism. Kim Il-sung was one of those Christians,[11] eventually creating the brutal totalitarian state that exists today.

Ultimately the slide into heresy and decline will either kill a movement, or the crises and decline created will lead to the kind of holy discontent that leads to a renewal dynamic. Without an immersion in the presence, the cycle begins again, often operating in different parts of the church simultaneously. Each extreme reacting to the other. Repelled by the descent into heresy of some of their fellow Christians, some will react by pushing further into religiosity, which only forces those drifting into irreligiosity further into their heresies.

> It is important to understand that many who are disillusioned with, or even repelled by, Christianity are in reality only disillusioned with or repelled by dead orthodoxy, worldly Christianity, or cultural Christianity.

BAPTIZING RENEWAL

Understanding these dynamics, we can see how our system trends toward decline. We see the desperate need for renewal, yet we can also sympathize with William J. Abraham when he cautions us that "renewal then is often a paradoxical affair. It is a sobering thought to ponder that sometimes our best efforts wreak havoc in the body of Christ." The flesh can become enflamed as the energies of renewal are released. Therefore, we can understand when Abraham warns us that "often, the medicine does more than we intended. Again and again leading personalities or major movements have appeared who have identified some deep problem in the life of the church. They propose and implement a solution. The solution then takes on a life of its own, so that across the generations it has led to other, equally serious problems."[12] One can't but help wonder if renewal itself needs a renewal, a baptism in the presence, in order to be washed clean of the workings of the flesh. Despite his soberness about the history of renewal, Abraham still urges the church to engage in a "long-haul, persistent, cross-generational renewal."[13]

But what would that look like our in our moment?

Chapter 9

Preparing for Renewal

Breaking Down before Building Up

Author L. P. Hartley famously wrote that the "the past is a foreign country: they do things differently there."[1] There is truth in Hartley's observation. Yet, while the past has differences, it also has similarities and analogies, which, when it comes to renewal, offer hope to those wishing for spiritual breakthrough in our current cultural moment. As I write, on my desk is George Marsden's biography of the theologian and preacher Jonathan Edwards. Its cover features a rather austere and stern looking Edwards, dressed in eighteenth-century garb, and regally holding a feather quill. Examining this image, one can imagine the revival of Christianity he was central to as occurring on another planet.

Yet upon closer examination, the great awakening of faith that Edwards experienced contains some intriguing parallels to our day. It began primarily among young adults of Northampton, Massachusetts, who lived during what Marsden notes was a cultural, economic, and social shift from a communal to a capitalist society. This meant that young people, unable to afford homes and farms, were delaying marriage, resulting in a generation gap and growth in sexual promiscuity. Northampton gained a reputation as a party town.

The strong community bonds that forged belonging and meaning were frayed, the mental and spiritual health of the young adults deteriorated; melancholy and depression were normative. The young adults were what Gertrude Stein would later label as a "lost generation"[2]—those who come of age in a time of change and uncertainty. Yet Edwards's patient ministry would result in a sovereign act of God; the young adults of Northampton would be the vanguard of a new move of God, which would soon move across generational, economic, traditional, and ethnic lines. "What had once seemed a valley of dry bones now flourished with spiritual life," Marsden writes.[3] This seemingly fallow ground would act as one of the vital sprigs in the transatlantic growth of faith known as the Great Awakening. We learn from Edwards's experience that renewal occurs when people get to the end of themselves, when the social bonds that have kept us strong begin to break, when the stories we have told to explain the world no longer make sense.

RENEWAL HAPPENS WHEN WE GET TO THE END OF OURSELVES

Cultural exhaustion opens the doorways to the human heart. When the cultural scripts we live by are exposed as frauds, delivering bad fruit, new possibilities begin to emerge. We are approaching such a moment in the West. For many of us, this is not an abstract idea. We are shaped by the faulty script as much as anyone; we ourselves are culturally exhausted, hitting or coming upon rock bottom. This is the perfect place to start again, when renewal is no longer an option, but our only hope left.

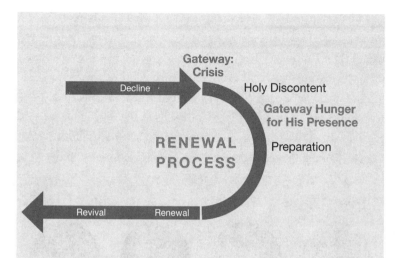

KEY RENEWAL PRINCIPLE
If you are at the end of yourself, you are ripe for a renewal.

Renewal comes when we are sickened by our false gods and the broken promises of our impotent idols and ideologies. When we are shattered by our striving and pathetic attempts at saving ourselves, we fall into the arms of Christ to be remade without caveats and compromises.

Exhausted and emptied, we can be filled by Him.

This, however, is something easier said than done. For blockages lie in the way of the road to renewal.

WE ARE POOR RECRUITS FOR RENEWAL

The Western life system has formed us in a particular way that creates people who resist the move of God in subconscious ways. The average Westerner is a radical individualist who is deeply afraid of compromising their autonomy. He or she determines their self-worth and identity primarily horizontally, via the media, culture, or peers. We are shaped by the passive-aggressive tone of consumerism, where we want maximum say with minimum responsibility. We are shaped primarily by our fluid and ever-shifting feelings. We yearn for community and connection, yet fear commitment and consistency. We wish for justice while desiring hedonistic payoffs. We religiously point the finger at others while jealously guarding our own right to do as we please. All these factors place us in a spiritually precarious place.

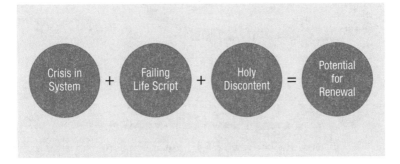

The hard truth is that even when we come to the end of ourselves, stepping into a holy discontent with our culture, these patterns have deeply shaped us. They have turned us into the kind of people who are useless in the kind of renewals and revivals that God brings, who most likely will resist renewal.

> Living in the deforming, anti-renewal life system of the West, we are shaped in such a distorted way that we are poor recruits for renewal. Yet, the first step is realizing how poorly prepared we are. How weak we really are.

WE MUST REALIZE OUR WEAKNESS

When we read the histories of those who God used powerfully in moments of renewal and revival, we see that they were not always those who were the most talented, connected, or charismatic; rather, they had all come to the end of themselves. Reflecting on this pattern, Martyn Lloyd-Jones writes,

> Read the histories and accounts of every revival that has ever taken place and you will invariably find this, that the one man or the group, the little group of people, who have been used in this way by God to send revival, have always known a state of utter desperation and final despair. Every single one of them. Read the journals of Whitefield and Wesley. Read the life history of all these men. They have always come to this place where they have realised their utter and absolute impotence. Their final paralysis. There is the Red Sea. Here is the enemy. There are the mountains. They are shut in, they are shut down, they are crushed to their knees. It is always the prerequisite. It is always the moment at which God acts.[4]

Lloyd-Jones wrote those words in midtwentieth-century Britain, in which post-Christianity was a fast approaching specter. His concern was that the seeming health of the church of his day would leave Christians too self-satisfied and comfortable to reach the depths of personal desperation that produces fuel for renewal.

Today, however, the post-Christianity Lloyd-Jones saw hovering on the horizon is now everywhere, distributing desperation widely— a desperation that creates fuel for renewal, opening up a world of new possibilities and potentials for God to move among a whole new generation that has reached what Lloyd-Jones called "their final paralysis."

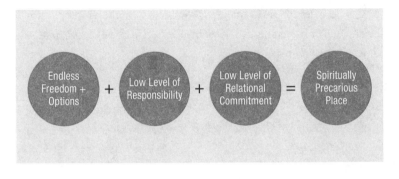

TAKE PERSONAL RESPONSIBILITY FOR RENEWAL BY NO LONGER TOLERATING YOURSELF AS YOU ARE

A person lost and drowning in the sea still has to make the decision to reach out and grasp the hand of a rescuer. Residents of rock bottom possess a strange ability to resist rescue and renewal and instead choose the better-known devil, wrapping themselves in the familiarity of dysfunction and despair.

KEY RENEWAL PRINCIPLE
For renewal to truly come, we must first reach the point where we make a choice to no longer tolerate our current state of being.

When we begin to channel a holy discontent, it is easy to channel it in other directions. All of us can find things in our culture or within the church that fuel a holy discontent, yet those who have come to the end of themselves, who hunger for God to again move, must first turn their holy discontent upon themselves. Not in self-condemnation, self-hatred, or insecurity, but rather in a courageous act of imagination.

> We are yet to see humans fully transformed by God,
> and won't till heaven. Therefore we are limited by a lack
> of imagination of what we can be in Christ—and we
> make this lack of imagination authoritative.

We must make the decision to no longer tolerate our low level of faith, our personal dysfunction, and give ourselves over to God's burning desire to remake us in Christlikeness.

> Only Christ can change us, but we must take
> responsibility for choosing to be changed.

Decide to truly embrace the truth that God gives His Spirit to those who obey Him (Acts 5:32). This a difficult task, for we are shaped by a culture of consumerism and spectatorship. We expect to be able to lob our opinion into any situation. We favor rights over responsibility. Christ has given authority; the Spirit is with us. Yet we must choose to move from a posture of passivity into proactivity, taking the hand of God as He leads us into His kingdom.

RENEWAL HAPPENS WHEN WE ENCOUNTER THE TRUE NATURE OF GOD AND FIND OUR INDIVIDUALISM DISPLACED

Having tasted the bitter fruit of radical individualism, we begin to shift our gaze from ourselves to God. This is a move that the devil will attempt to ferociously undermine. Having plunged us into the miry clay, the enemy wishes us to stay there. He hopes we will not look heavenward in desperation but instead glance horizontally, searching for false answers and earthly justifications for a spiritually fruitless life. For Satan is in the game of diminishing expectations. Our cultural architecture aids this quest. Our culture of digital consumption constantly forms us into a posture of passivity. Our drive to ever-increasing individual autonomy ironically leads us to herdlike behavior.

We carry the burden and anxiety of being our own bosses, looking left and right for earthly guidance, leadership, and standards. Sadly, Christians are just as prone to this temptation as anyone else, resulting in our reduced concept of God, His power and holiness reoriented around earthly standards. Instead, when we reach that holy place of coming to the end of ourselves, we shift our view from the horizontal plane of earthly standards, adjusting vertically to recognize God's concepts of holiness, justice, and righteousness. We choose to displace our own authority, subvert our radical individualism.

KEY RENEWAL PRINCIPLE
Renewal happens when we step into the freedom of following.

A DIFFERENT KIND OF INDIVIDUALISM

Here we encounter a different kind of individualism, where the world falls away for a moment, and we stand before Him alone. Freed from the rule of the crowd, from our instinct to anxiously herd into the group-think, from the buzz of constant distraction, we turn from the faces of those around us to look upon His face.

As we do this, we begin to grasp who He really is, and strangely as we look toward God, our true selves come into clear view. We are struck by how far we fall short of Him, how we have tried to re-mold Him in our own image; our pitiable games at playing god are exposed, the ruse of radical individualism is shown for the fraud it is. Just at the moment when, in comparison to God, it seems that we as humans could not shrink any smaller, the divine hand of grace reaches out to remake us. Shocked by the seeming incongruence of such a moment, we find ourselves again standing before the paradox of the cross, in which justice and love are held together.

We must grasp our smallness before God can use us to do big things.

Every renewal and revival begins with people who reach such a moment, who truly come to the end of themselves, discovering the depth of their own sin and the immensity of a holy God who is intent on removing rebellion, evil, and ill from the world, yet who sent His Son to die upon the cross to invite us to be on His side in the remaking of the world. Such moments then become seeds planted in harvest.

No longer do we face the heavy task of defining ourselves, of crafting our own identity; instead, He will do that now, when we fully give ourselves over to Him.

He will begin molding us into a redeemed version of ourselves we could never believe possible. For He wishes to shape us, so we can return to our original purpose of partnering with Him in His plan to move history to His purposes, flooding the world with His presence.

PERSONAL RENEWAL IS FRIENDSHIP WITH GOD

"It is time for you, noble friend, to be known by God and to become his friend,"[5] wrote the early church father Gregory of Nyssa. This is the root of personal renewal—a friendship with God. Jesus' death on the cross tears the curtain in the temple, which kept His presence quarantined from the world. With Jesus' sacrificial death, He wishes to again fill His temple with His presence. Yet this side of Jesus' death and resurrection, the temple is not the structure that was destroyed by the Roman armies in the year AD 70. Your body is a living temple. His plan is to fill the world again, His cosmic temple with His presence— that is the end point of history. During this act of His great drama, He moves history toward His purposes by filling us with His presence.

KEY RENEWAL PRINCIPLE
The renewal of our post-Christian societies begins
with acts of personal desecularizing.

THE IDOLS MUST BE REMOVED FROM YOUR TEMPLE

The false gods that fill our personal temples must be removed, the barred rooms reserved for our personal autonomy must be opened up, the keys must be handed over. His presence must be invited to flood in, filling every inch of our lives. For our goal is not self-actualization, nor self-expression; rather, it is life with God. Life with the presence. We must decrease, so He can increase. For as we decrease, we become more filled with His presence, taking His presence with us into our lives, into the web of relationships in which we move, the places we visit, the moments in time we inhabit. Yet to do this, we must be first changed by the coming of His presence.

THE SEARCHING, SCORCHING MANIFESTATION OF PRESENCE

Renewals are simply a way in which God moves His plan toward completion. J. I. Packer writes that "it is with this searching, scorching manifestation of God's presence that renewal begins, and by its continuance that renewal is sustained."[6] His presence is both the destination and the road. As His presence comes among us during renewal, our flesh—that part of us which wishes for autonomy, to achieve our own kingdom separate from God—is confronted. It feels the scorching of His presence.

KEY RENEWAL PRINCIPLE
Renewal will go to war with our flesh, increasing
His presence in our lives.

This can happen on both a personal and corporate level as God shapes and prepares us for the end of history when His presence will fill the earth, and to mold us into agents of His presence in the world, partnering with Him in His renewal plans.

HOLINESS

God is holy, and so are His dwelling places. His temples—our lives, the church, or creation—must be filled with His holiness. In 1904, a revival touched Wales. Upwards of 100,000 people came to faith in an outpouring of God's presence that radically changed the face of the country. A crucial spark that lit the fire of revival occurred when a young man named Evan Roberts prayed with a small group of young people after a service. He felt the Lord challenging them to do the following:

> 1. *You must put away any unconfessed sin.*
> 2. *You must put away any doubtful habit.*
> 3. *You must obey the Spirit promptly.*
> 4. *You must confess Christ publicly.*[7]

All seventeen responded, choosing the way of holiness. This quiet and sacred moment, a foundation, must be seen in relation to the incredible and visible victories that occurred in the large-scale move of God across Wales. For renewal cannot come without holiness. God wishes to rid His temples of what does not please Him.

CONVICTION

We recently renovated our home. Our backyard was dug up, and a truckload of fresh, rich, fertile soil was brought in. We sowed into the ground a bag of expensive grass seed to ensure a lush lawn. However, it was summer, and the scorching sun was arriving. Apart from a few areas, the grass struggled to grow. Months later, the grass still was in patches, and the fertile rich soil had hardened into a grassless surface.

My suggested solution was simply to buy some more seed online and throw it on the hardened ground. Much wiser was my wife, who went out one afternoon with a rake, breaking and digging up the hardened soil. It was an act of destruction that had to precede the creation to come. If I had gone ahead with my foolish plan, the seed would have sat on top of the hardened layer of earth, only to wash away when the rains came. Before His rains of blessing and renewal come, the spoil must be broken up, turned over, so we can be ready to receive.

> **KEY RENEWAL PRINCIPLE**
> **In renewal, the breaking down must come
> before the building up.**

Hardened soil must be turned back into fertile earth. God prepares the soil of heart by sending His presence to convict us.

As God's holy presence comes among us, because it comes to fight the flesh, a conviction regarding sin will be felt strongly. In light of His presence, what was accepted before can no longer be tolerated. Sin must be discovered and exposed to the light of His coming. When this happens, "it is time to cease excusing our sins by calling them shortcomings or natural weakness, or by attributing them to temperament or environment. It is time to cease justifying our carnal ways and materialistic outlook by pointing to others who are the same," writes Arthur Wallis, noting that we must step into this conviction, which removes the way in which our flesh is resisting His Spirit, for "we must face our sins honestly in the light of God's Word, view them as He does and deal with them as before Him. Until we do, it would be well that God should withhold the rain of revival."[8]

> **KEY RENEWAL PRINCIPLE**
> If renewal comes upon unprepared hearts,
> it will simply wash away.

CONFESSION FOLLOWS CONVICTION

Conviction can be met with defensiveness and avoidance, or even the temptation of self-condemnation, yet its true partner is confession. When God lovingly shines a light on an area in which we fall short of His standards, it is an act of mercy.

> The divine sword comes, but its intent is to cut us free
> of the net that ensnares our hearts.

For as James instructs, confession brings spiritual power and effectiveness: "Confess your sins to each other and pray for each other so that you may be healed. The prayer of a righteous person is powerful and effective" (James 5:16).

REPENTANCE FOLLOWS CONFESSION

Confession must be accompanied with repentance. As Paul writes to the church in Corinth, "Godly sorrow brings repentance that leads to salvation and leaves no regret, but worldly sorrow brings death" (2 Cor. 7:10). Those who are to enter His kingdom must pass through the door of repentance. Repentance is a whole life change, a commitment to put aside our own pattern of behavior or thought and to align with God's desire for redemption and reconciliation.

In the last days of World War II, Basilea Schlink led German Christian youth into sustained prayers of repentance for their nation's sins. Despite their city being engulfed in a devastating battle, Schlink and the young people she led experienced renewal in the midst of the brutal combat, recounting:

In the months following the destruction of our city everyone was filled
with fear and terror. . . . But we experienced that heaven was close to
us, especially when we had a retreat with the young people for several
days while the battle raged on . . . the perils of war vanished before the
reality of heaven.

Schlink discovered the essential link between renewal and repentance, reflecting: "I had the privilege of tasting the renewed life and joy that came from contrition and repentance."[9]

> ### KEY RENEWAL PRINCIPLE
> **Repentance and renewal are inseparable companions.**

PERSONAL RENEWAL LEADS TO CORPORATE CHANGE[10]

As God renews individuals who are embedded within a dysfunctional and despairing culture, they act as antibodies, agents of the King with the potential to renew a whole culture. They are influencers, often prayed for by the people of God, as Richard F. Lovelace reminds us: "Redemption comes under the direction of leaders whom God raises up in his sovereign mercy in response to the deep longing and intercession of the laity generated under the pressure of defeat or suffering."[11]

Your personal renewal is the answer to the prayers of people grieved by our true state and desperate for God to again move in our time. For renewal gives us new, holy, and healing leaders and influencers.

The church begins when a disparate and dishevelled group of very ordinary people, crying out to God, are filled with His presence. This handful of renewed people, with no army, no political power, and little funds, would turn the world upside down. At every moment the church has been renewed and revived, we discover the same phenomenon—a person or a handful of people who have gotten to the end of themselves, who cannot tolerate it anymore, who fall at the feet of Christ and are filled with His presence, who become infectious agents of the kingdom in the world. Contenders for His renewal.

Chapter 10

From Consuming to Contending

The Sacrificial, Risk-Taking,
Responsibility-Embracing Posture of Renewal

Up to this point, our journey through the cycle of renewal has been one of preparation. Now the phase begins in which the inner work begins to radiate outward, in which we choose to align ourselves proactively with God's agenda of renewal in the world. Contending for God's plan of renewal. To contend is to battle, stretch, or reach for something. To step into the phase of contending renewal requires the shedding of the life posture of consumer.

CONSUMER CHRISTIANITY

Many of us may balk at forms of cultural Christianity that mix nationalism or ethnic identity and faith, yet we miss how we have been shaped by our own dominant culture, the culture of consumerism. Consumer culture is placeless, yet pervasive. It is the water in which we swim.

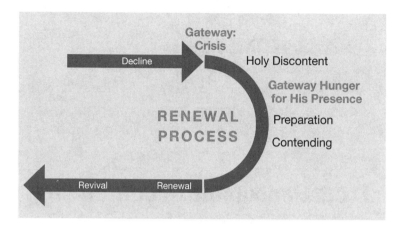

Consumer Christianity is a form of cultural Christianity that compromises the cross with self rather than flag, mixing the worship of God with the worship of options, personal autonomy, low commitment, and opinion over responsibility.

Consumer culture tells us we can do it all, yet we become paralyzed by endless options. FOMO, the fear of missing out, according to author Patrick McGinnis, is now accompanied by FOBO, the fear of better options: "I noticed that my classmates and I were always optimizing. We hedged, lived in a world of maybes and were paralyzed at the prospect of actually committing to something, out of fear that we might be choosing something that wasn't the absolutely perfect option."[1] McGinnis reports that the fear of better options leads ultimately to the fear of doing anything. Unlimited options and the search for lifestyle perfection leaves us paralyzed. And paralysis prevents renewal.

KEY RENEWAL PRINCIPLE
Renewal comes when we choose to walk the one truth path.

CONSUMERISM WITHOUT LIMITS LEADS TO PARALYSIS

Crushed by the pressure that we should be doing it all with perfection, we fall into passivity, frozen with choice anxiety and the pressure to perform. It can feel easier to not try at all. Better to sit on the couch and throw critique without consequence at those who are trying to achieve, while simultaneously experiencing jealousy of those who seem to reach lifestyle success. We become caught in a vicious cycle of trying to fulfill the desires that consumer culture places in us, trying to do it all, then retreating in fear of doing anything. We cycle between running ourselves ragged and then retreating to the couch to binge on Netflix and Uber Eats. Never working well, nor resting well. Passive-aggressive because we never confront our frustrations directly. Instead we become trapped in our own feelings and anxiety of getting it wrong, protecting ourselves with a brittle veneer of confidence. Unconsciously, we continually shift blame to others for our own lack of growth, then circle back to condemning ourselves for our inability to achieve the lifestyle we desire.

TOXIC ENTITLEMENT

Consumer culture creates in us a mentality of toxic entitlement—the sense that we can have it all, but without struggle or cost. This mentality of entitlement eventually will infect our faith. As John Townsend warns, it "directs us to judge God for how the world works, for the bad things that happen to us that we don't understand, and for things that didn't happen that we desired."[2] The Christian caught in consumer Christianity shifts blame for their lack of growth to God, their leaders, the church, their friends, spouse, or family, insulating themselves against renewal. We fool ourselves that someone else will solve the problem of our lack of discipleship.

The good news is that we are reaching the limits of a consumer culture without limits. The possibility of living out of the passive posture of consumerism is passing as its negative effects are felt. Churches and faith built on consumerism don't last beyond a generation.

CHOOSING TO CONTEND

When we step into the posture of contending, we choose to stand in the place of transformation rather than accumulation. We no longer live to acquire a portfolio of possessions and cool experiences. Instead, the horizon we are heading for, which will shape our lives, is the meeting of heaven and earth at the end of the age. Consumer culture is driven by the myth of secularism, that there is nothing more than stuff—you are just stuff, so grab all the stuff you can before you die. In contrast, the posture of contending flows from the truth that there is a great divine drama at play, there is far more than just stuff. God invites us to partner with Him, contending, and centering our lives around His mission in the world. This is a truth that is not just affirmed—it is walked out. Nets must be dropped. We believe with our feet, each step a choice to contend rather than simply live to consume.

> The way out of the paralysis that endless consumerism creates is through following the Father's footsteps.

CONSUMERISM IS THE WORSHIP OF COMFORT AND AVOIDANCE OF DIFFICULTY

God uses the difficulties and suffering we encounter to reshape us. As Paul writes to the church in Rome, "We know that in all things God works for the good of those who love him, who have been called according to his purpose" (Rom. 8:28). Groaning, waiting, hungering for His kingdom to come in fullness, aligned with His plan to fill the world with His presence, becoming ambassadors and symbols of that future.

> **KEY RENEWAL PRINCIPLE**
> Renewal reframes all of our absences, our hurts,
> our disappointments, and as we turn back to Him,
> we are remade in holiness.

Contending is choosing to step into the hard places with God, joining creation's choir in groaning for our final liberation. Paul reminded the young Timothy that the good soldier does not get entangled in civilian affairs, but rather wishes to obey his commanding officer. Consumer Christianity thoroughly entangles us in civilian affairs. Contending is living to please our commanding officer, leaving behind the irrelevance of civilian concerns and the myth of finding a life of meaning in the avoidance of difficulty. Renewal always springs from the desert; the presence is encountered in the wilderness.

CONSUMERISM IS ABOUT THE EXTERNALS; CONTENDING IS ABOUT THE RENEWAL OF INTERNALS

Consumer culture disciples us to change our external situation through purchasing to bring pleasure, meaning, and happiness to our inner world. Contending takes the opposite approach. Personal renewals begin in the hidden places, often driven by solitary prayer and self-examination, communion with God, fasting and the habits of secrecy, the uprooting of sinful patterns, and confessions with trusted leaders and pastors. Eventually this inner change of the heart will overflow out into our external lives, creating a potential for renewal in the social world around us.

Jesus keenly understood this dynamic relationship between our inner and outer worlds, telling His disciples, "A good man brings good things out of the good stored up in his heart, and an evil man brings evil things out of the evil stored up in his heart. For the mouth speaks what the heart is full of" (Luke 6:45). Our words, our perspective, our attitudes and desires, and even our posture begin to change as Christ renews us, reshaping us in His image. Others notice this change, consciously or subconsciously. We present a challenge to those stuck within the pattern of the anti-renewal system in the form of a living example of a life-giving alternative.

> **KEY RENEWAL PRINCIPLE**
> **When we contend, we become champions of renewal.**

In contending, we understand that the process of inner renewal occurring within us is not just a project of self-actualization, but the fount of a blessing that spills over into the lives of others.

CONTENDING IS ABOUT TAKING RISKS AND EMBRACING RESPONSBILITY

Consumer culture trains us to sit back and wait for bargains and benefits. Loosely committing, letting others do the job. Consumer culture is risk-averse; it teaches us to run from responsibility, because it may reduce our options.

"We are witnessing a fundamental change," notes Nassim Nicholas Taleb, a fundamental social power shift, "the disappearance of a sense of heroism; a shift away from certain respect—and power— to those who take downside risks for others,"[3] a vital component of renewing a system. We need people who are prepared to sacrifice to improve the life-system of others, at great risk to themselves, people who realize that renewal will most likely encounter pain, difficulty, misunderstandings, and opposition, but who choose to move ahead regardless. For the health "of society depends on them; if we are here today, it is because someone, at some stage, took some risks for us," reflecting on those who have sacrificed to get us to this point, adding, "the word 'sacrifice' is related to *sacred*, the domain of the holy that is separate from that of the profane."[4]

> **Now the power has shifted from the risk-takers to those with no skin in the game—those with the loudest voices, who prefer comfort and commentary without consequence.**

Echoing Taleb's sentiment, Edwin Friedman, whose concepts of systemic renewal we explored in chapter 5, writes that those of us who are alive today "[benefit] from centuries of risk-taking by previous generations,"[5] a challenge that can equally be delivered to the contemporary church in the West, built on the contending of previous generations for renewal. Friedman's comment that we run the risk today of morphing into a society of "'skimmers' who constantly take from the top without adding significantly to its essence"[6] can also be applied to contemporary Christianity.

> **KEY RENEWAL PRINCIPLE**
> Contenders refuse to accept opinion without responsibility, commentary without action. They choose to count the cost. They dive deep into commitment. They know that Christ is with them and that His renewal is the only truly safe place in the world.

RENEWALS BUILD UPON THE POWER OF PERSEVERING

Instant gratification is essential to consumer culture. We are formed not only to desire but to desire *now*, taught that if we have to wait it is not worth it. This framework can shape how we view renewal. Many, initially excited and encouraged by the first sprigs of renewal, will soon change their tune when the sacrifice and patience required become apparent.

Friedman cautions those engaged in the task of renewal: "A major difficulty in sustaining one's mission is that others who start out with the same enthusiasm will come to lose their nerve. Mutiny and sabotage came not from enemies who opposed the initial idea, but rather from colleagues whose will was sapped by unexpected hardships along the way."

When opposition, misunderstanding, and isolation come to those contending for renewal, we should expect it. Arthur Wallis writes,

> We must be miniature forerunners, each in our own sphere. It is not enough to prepare the way in our own hearts; we must prepare the way in the hearts of others. This is a ministry which demands steadfastness of purpose, desire and expectancy, for it is fraught with disappointments. Some seem to catch the vision at once, but setbacks, delays or opposition take their toll, and they lose that vision.[7]

When this happens, we have the opportunity to reframe the difficulty as an opportunity to push further into God's presence, to dwell closer to the Vine. With our God-given courage, when we stay the course, remaining among those who may be rejecting the renewal in us, meeting their opposition with kindness, humility, and holy fortitude, our perseverance will build character within us.

KEY RENEWAL PRINCIPLE
Perseverance builds character. Character builds spiritual authority. Spiritual authority builds influence. Influence spreads the renewal.

Spiritual authority is God-given influence, an ability to move others toward God's purposes, not through human powers of motivation, but through a holy life that flows outward. As we surrender our wills, we become tools in His hands, agents of His influence.

CONTENDING FOR SACRED SPACE IN THE WORLD

One of the great intents of contemporary Christianity of the last few decades has been to tear down the false division between the sacred and the secular. That is, to reject the idea that some activities such as singing hymns or praying can be holy, while others, such as baking a cake or swimming, are profane. This was a necessary correction. However, it has often been crudely applied, morphing into an approach that enables the Christian to uncritically wade into every activity and place, proclaiming them all holy. Such an approach in a culture of consumerism, which views hedonism as the ultimate good, can rapidly dissolve faith.

Scripture does not divide the world into sacred and profane activities. It addresses the breadth of human life, from mildew to the gift of exhortation, yet it does not proclaim everything holy or sacred. Yes, the end of the story sees the world redeemed, filled with God's holiness and glory. However, when it comes to the time in which we live, Scripture paints our lives as being engaged in a struggle, not against flesh and blood but against spiritual powers and principalities. Fallen forces that occupy ground. Michael S. Heiser writes, "Believers today are in a spiritual war. We are now God's temple, the special place God's Spirit resides, points of the light of his presence—and we are scattered throughout a world in bondage to the powers of darkness."[8] We are temples of the Holy Spirit individually, but not in isolation; the church (locally and universally) is also a temple of the Holy Spirit, not bound to one location. Through Jesus' sacrificial death upon the cross, He has renewed our mandate to spread the presence of God in the world.

KEY RENEWAL PRINCIPLE
As we contend, we partner with God, carving out
sacred space in the world.

Jesus told His followers that where only two or three are gathered in His name, there His presence is. Reflecting on Jesus' words in their biblical context, Heiser observes that "viewed in the context of the Old Testament idea of sacred space, that statement means that wherever believers gather, the spiritual ground they occupy is sanctified amid the powers of darkness."[9] This means that as we contend, crying out to God, worshiping Him, we carve out sacred space in our rooms, our homes, our streets, our schools, our workplaces, our cities, our nations, our world.

As we walk into the posture of contending, we discover habits, forms, and practices that aid renewal. Fertile patterns that bring new life. It is the role these renewal patterns play that we turn to next.

Chapter II

Repatterning for Renewal

Cultivating Faith in the West's Secular Mega-Temple

France's national identity is deeply enmeshed with its concept of *laïcité*, the secular separation of church and state, a clear curtain between private belief and the public realm. This idea bounces around my mind as I step off the cobblestoned streets of the regional city of Tours and into the Basilica of St. Martin. The church was built to celebrate the life of the fourth-century Christian leader Martin of Tours, who left his post as a Roman soldier to lead a renewal that would turn the Roman city of Tours into an evangelistic hub within Europe.

I move from the main worship space and climb the stairs down into the burial place of Martin. It's winter, and the temperature drops as I descend into the tomb. Underneath the church, beneath the city, in this small room that feels like a freezer, it is almost as if this pioneer of renewal has been frozen in France's secular soil, a marker of another time in which public faith and private belief were not so neatly sliced apart. The church around me is a representation of the way in which the renewal that Martin's evangelistic monastic community of late antiquity had marked this city, its identity, and its patterns. The French revolutionaries understood the power of such buildings to mark out the patterns of a population, destroying the original church that marked the memory of Martin of Tours. For these revolutionaries, eager to set about their own post-Christian order, the cathedrals of Europe were a kind of propaganda set in stone, which must be countered.

THE CATHEDRAL OF PATTERNS

Reflecting on the awe-inspiring grandeur of the medieval cathedral seen by worshipers in the Middle Ages, the art historian E. H. Gombrich wrote,

> Today it is not easy to imagine what a church meant to the people of that period. Only in some old villages in the countryside can we still get a glimpse of its importance. The church was often the only stone building anywhere in the neighbourhood; it was the only considerable structure for miles around, and its steeple was a landmark to all who approached from afar. On Sundays and during services all the inhabitants of the town might meet there, and the contrast between the lofty building with its paintings and carving and the private and humble dwellings in which these people spent their lives must have been overwhelming."[1]

The cathedrals were created as three dimensional teaching tools, built by a community over generations to orientate themselves toward the end point of an eternity with God.

RENEWAL IN THE SECULAR MEGA-TEMPLE

As Gombrich illuminates, towering over everything else, the medieval cathedral's power was staggering. Its bells, liturgy, and rhythms defining not just what happened within the church walls but outside of it, as it shaped the very patterns of time, both for individuals and the community. Today, we are also overwhelmed, not by cathedrals, but by even more powerful creations that are designed to orientate us toward a goal by shaping our patterns. The whole of contemporary Western culture—from the structure of our malls and cities, to the very fabric of the internet and social media platforms—are ideologies that shape us toward a vision not rooted in the eternal, but in the unlimited freedom and pleasure of the individual.

> Western culture, then, is a kind of giant secular cathedral, a globalizing mega-temple oriented around post-Christian worship, which shapes us at profound, and unconscious levels, leading us away from renewal, and toward personal and corporate decline.

To act as agents of renewal, we must examine how we can reorient our life-systems toward God's plan to fill the world with His presence. How do we live and worship faithfully while surrounded by an immersive secular mega-temple? We do so by transforming the patterns that influence our lives into worship of God. To do this, we must understand how patterns work.

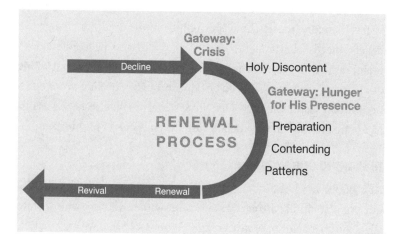

THE PATTERN DYNAMIC

First, let's define what I am calling patterns. Psychologist Daniel Goleman notes that "our brain has two semi-independent, largely separate mental systems."[2] These systems run at separate speeds. Our slower brain system is aware of the decisions it makes; it is where our self-control and willpower exist. It chooses to focus its attention on singular items, such as what we are engaged in consciously in that moment. Our faster brain system runs on autopilot. It deals in the background with the incredible volume of stimulation that our senses deal with at any moment. For example, most likely you are reading this book sitting down, your slower brain concentrating on the words and concepts. Stop and become aware of the kind of seat you are sitting in. Note the sensation of what you are sitting on. Become aware of how the chair, sofa, or subway is interacting with your skin and muscles in your thighs, lower back, and buttocks. Your slower brain has just switched its attention to these stimuli. Before, your faster brain was filtering them out so you could focus your attention on this book.

Your faster brain is driven by desires, impulses, and emotions. It is also the command center of our habits, driving our behavior and actions. Therefore, those who wish to influence us need not change our beliefs, that is, the thoughts of our conscious and deliberate slower brain; rather, they need to influence our faster brain, thus controlling our habits and actions. This can be done through appealing to our emotions, desires, and longings. Our life systems are then reshaped as our habits are hijacked and pointed toward the end goals of big business.

HIJACKING OUR HABITS

At a public level, the stories that we tell about ourselves in much of our popular culture are at complete odds with how those who wish to shape our behavior operate in reality. We are told that we are creative, original, and spontaneous individuals, believing that we choose what to think, believe, desire, and feel. Such a vision appeals to our slower brain, which believes that it is in ultimate control.

Yet in reality, with their keen and highly pragmatic understanding of human nature, those who wish to shape us treat us very differently. We are understood as predictable creatures, deeply influenced by the crowd. We view ourselves as spontaneous, yet we are easily shaped by simple cues and basic psychological tricks, manipulated by those who are able to hijack our habits. Just think of the countless people who wish to be healthy and yet find themselves purchasing junk food when their emotions drop, or those who morally and philosophically oppose pornography yet are addicted. Just think of how many times a day you reach for your phone for no reason.

With that foundation of understanding established, what I mean by a pattern is this:

PATTERNS: The inputs, habits, and rituals that shape our personal life architecture, determining the health of our life system.

Vast amounts of time and money are spent by corporations and tech giants to arrange our life architecture to suit their goals. The life system of the average person in the West is now primarily shaped around the patterns set by our phones to harvest information to be sold for profit, as well as influencing us to purchase particular goods and experiences. Our life patterns have become one of the great battlegrounds of the contemporary world.

POINTING OUR PATTERNS TOWARD HEAVEN

Ultimately our patterns determine the health of our life-system. When we return to the biblical vision for humanity, we see that we are created to worship and, as we learned in chapter 5, commissioned with a purpose to spread God's presence in the world, until His glory covers the earth.

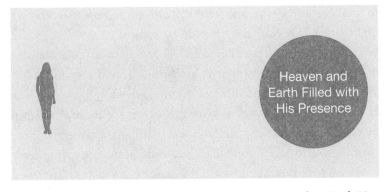

We are built with this longing in our hearts to worship God. Humans are created to follow, love, serve, submit, and worship. Yet God doesn't simply ask us to sit back while He accomplishes this task. He invites us to partner with Him.

We therefore are also created to shape the world while we are reshaped ourselves for God's purposes. God achieves this through the patterns of worship in our lives.

Alexander Schmemann writes that "the first, the basic definition of a man is that he is *the priest*. He stands in the center of the world and unifies it in his act of blessing God, of both receiving the world from God and offering it God." By living this life of total worship, "he transforms his life, the one that he receives from the world, into life in God, into communion with him."[3] Therefore, when we are living as God's children—submitted to Him, following Jesus and His way— our patterns of worship, our receiving the world from God, and giving it back to Him as an act of worship, will reflect God's end goals and shape us for where we are going with God, and where we will dwell for eternity. We are shaped by where we are going, which ultimately leads us to worship and love God.

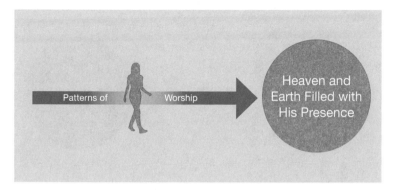

However, when we do not follow God, when our lives are not submitted to His will, we pattern our lives around our loves. We still worship, but what we are worshiping is not God. Schmemann warns that "when we see the world as an end in itself, everything becomes itself a value and consequently loses all value, because only in God is found the meaning (value) of everything, and the world is meaningful only when it is the 'sacrament' of God's presence. Things treated merely as things in themselves destroy themselves because only in God have they any life."[4] Meaning leaks out of life. We replace God with other things, or in the biblical language, idols. In the contemporary West, these idols are less likely to be carvings of stone and wood, but rather visions of individual pleasure, freedom, and autonomy as the ultimate good. This is a faulty and flawed vision, in which Schmemann laments that the human "ceased to be the priest of the world and became its slave."[5]

Our worship, the patterns of our lives, will be reshaped around our disordered desires, engineering us at deep and powerful levels, directing us away from God.

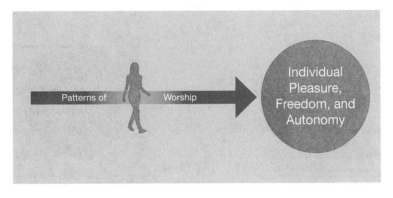

WISHING FOR RENEWAL VERSUS PATTERNING TOWARD RENEWAL

To understand how we can reorient our patterns toward God, reengaging with our priestly posture, we must understand the role that our longings and desires play in our patterns of life. James K. A. Smith writes, "We are orientated by our longings, directed by our desires. We adopt ways of life that are indexed to such visions of the good life, not usually because we 'think through' our options."[6] Notice that Smith says we do not think our way through this. Our thoughts and beliefs can be in contrast or even opposition to our patterns of behavior. Instead, "we get pulled into a way of life," Smith notes, which has power to shape us, "not by convincing the intellect, but by allure."[7] This is a key insight.

> We can wish and desire for renewal yet do so
> with divided hearts, thus living out patterns of worship
> that undermine renewal.

We can affirm God's plan and purposes with our words, intentions, and beliefs, we can sing worship songs with all our hearts in church, but our life patterns can lead us to a very different end, trending us away from renewal.

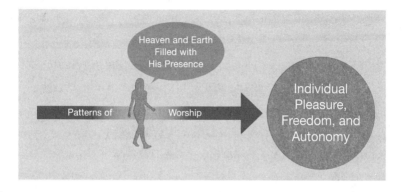

SACRIFICIAL LAMBS ON THE ALTAR OF THE SECULAR MEGA-TEMPLE

The cost of following these futile patterns means that we become the sacrificial lambs to our dysfunctional society, which drives us to achieve while undermining us. Our relationships, our communities, the church—these are sacrificed at the altar of radical individualism. As Dallas Willard reminds us, "Sacrifice in religious ritual signals the effects of our failure to do what we were meant to do—whatever else its point."[8] However, when God is central, when His presence is close, when our patterns of worship move us toward Him, we engage in a different kind of sacrifice.

As Paul states in his letter to the church in Rome, "To offer your bodies as a living sacrifice, holy and pleasing to God—this is your true and proper worship. Do not conform to the pattern of this world, but be transformed by the renewing of your mind" (Rom. 12:1–2). Our patterns of worship, how we live out the good news with our bodies, is our sacrifice, one that does not destroy but renews the whole of our being, transforming our thoughts, emotions, and actions. As Tom Wright explains, "The habits of heart, mind, and life to which we are called are designed to form us, gradually and bit by bit, into people who can, with the hard-won 'second nature' that we call virtue, freely and gladly take forward these tasks."[9] Our life patterns, directed toward God, reshape us as agents of renewal in the world.

> **Patterns, therefore, which align us with how God has created the world can be called wise and essential to a flourishing life.**

Israel's priests were commanded to teach people the knowledge of God. Priests are teachers and exemplifiers of God's wisdom and ways. As followers of Jesus, renewal occurs when we take up our priestly role to live out and teach God's knowledge, directing our worship toward Him, through the patterns of our lives.

> **As priests in God's cosmic temple, we worship with the pattern of our lives.**

THE RENEWAL WE NEED

Here is where the renewal needed in the contemporary West will be different from many other renewals. Much of current church practice and models of church growth are built around a concept that people may enter our communities with a lack of belief, discipleship, and knowledge of God. We meet these needs through worship services, community groups, Bible study, and volunteering. All these programs assume a pattern of basic functioning and life skills. Sure, throughout history, churches have provided services and options for people from damaged backgrounds who needed extra care and assistance to integrate into community and functionality. However, as the anti-renewal script of the West reshapes the patterns of our lives in more invasive and powerful ways, dysfunction becomes normative. Poor mental health becomes standard fare for the majority, lack of emotional resilience commonplace, and the basic skills needed for human functioning absent from many.

These realities present significant challenges to our model of church as those who enter our communities and systems struggle with basic issues of life functionality. It doesn't matter if it is a megachurch filled with programs, a liturgical high church, or a missional house church—if those walking into your community see physical presence at your activities as a low priority, if they lack the emotional resilience to receive gentle instruction, or find it normal to pull out of a volunteer leadership task via text message with half an hour's notice—any church will struggle to function as growing numbers of people professing faith, yet shaped by the anti-renewal machine, join their community.

Increasingly, our programs of discipleship, community, and ministry are running aground due to this lack of basic life functionality.

The reality that we must face is that so much of the functionality and fruitfulness in the church and Christian world is emerging from people living out life patterns from a previous era, or from migrants living life patterns that emerge from contexts outside the West.

REBUILDING OUR PATTERNS

Alongside the patterns of spiritual disciplines and the practices of Christian community and worship, we need forming patterns that align those set adrift by the failing life system with reality. Therefore, we need three levels of patterns:

FORMING PATTERNS *align us with the reality of how humans and God's world work, integrating into our lives patterns of functionality and wisdom, which enable us to live flourishing lives. The biblical wisdom books offer a vast resource of patterns and direction with which to construct helpful patterns. Forming patterns involve learning* the importance of diligence, of matching our words and actions, of integrating into our lives the values of delaying gratification for greater goals and being responsible for the consequences of our actions. All these forming patterns occur as we interact with reality, as we enact daily godly and wise choices, which creates a pattern of formation in our lives, shaping us into healthy and well-functioning humans.

DISCIPLESHIP PATTERNS align us with God's kingdom, creating habits and disciplines in our lives that shape us for God's kingdom, shaping us into Christlikeness and Christlike community. Dallas Willard says that these discipleship disciplines "are activities of mind and body purposefully undertaken, to bring our personality and total being into effective cooperation with the divine order. They enable us more and more to live in a power that is, strictly speaking, beyond us, deriving from the spiritual realm itself."[10] We practice discipleship patterns as we apprentice ourselves to those who have lived knowledge of how to live lives within the kingdom of God. When we follow these people, imitating them as they imitate Christ, we step into a life of discipleship.

INFLUENCING PATTERNS align us with God's mission in the world, forming within us patterns that spread the presence of God into the whole world. These patterns take us beyond ourselves, reconnecting us with our mandate to spread God's presence in the world. We do this by sharing the good news of Jesus Christ, by serving the economically poor, and by operating in our vocations filled with the presence of God.

The renewal that we need in the West will see the establishment of these three vital levels of patterns.

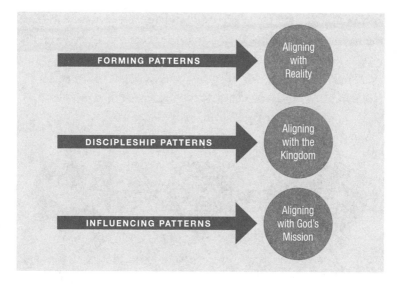

PATTERNS AID US IN CREATING AN ENVIRONMENT THAT SUPPORTS RENEWAL RATHER THAN WORKS AGAINST IT

As a life of contention is lived, the presence lives more fully in our personal life-system. We discover the power of the spiritual disciplines as more than just additions to our personal life goals, but rather central pillars and walls in the building of a new life architecture. Biblical faith deals with the "architecture of time,"[11] thus as we recenter our lives around God's presence, we reorder around a different time scale.

KEY RENEWAL PRINCIPLE

We must allow eternity to reshape our life patterns. Do this, and the fabric of our lives will be oriented around renewal.

Patterns are the building blocks of our life systems. As we are renewed, these building blocks shift from being driven by corporate wants to the patterns of the kingdom of God. Our renewal patterns anchor us to the ways in which God brought His presence in the past, the fruitful patterns that have sustained the church throughout history. Imitation is central to the reformation of our patterns. Yet they also direct us to the future; they are patterns of intent, which act as a plumb line to renewal that God wishes to bring in the future.

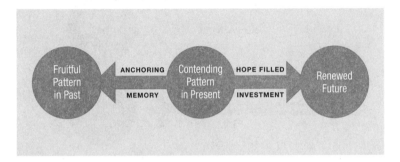

PATTERNS ARE THE SEEDS OF RENEWAL

To reform our life patterns toward renewal, to initiate life-giving, renewing, Christ-focused habits and practices, is an investment into the future that God wishes to bring.

KEY RENEWAL PRINCIPLE
God-focused patterns lived today are seeds planted, to be reaped in tomorrow's harvest of renewal.

Holy patterns push us beyond the limited and failing script of radical individualism into Christian community and fellowship. A community of renewal—a remnant—is one of the great patterns that has brought renewal in the past and offers a way forward for the renewals to come.

Chapter 12

Remnants—The Cells of Renewal

How Small Groups Lead to Big Renewals

When a devastating plague hit the German town of Glaucha in 1682, two-thirds of the population perished. The fabric of society was ripped apart, and soon poverty followed in the footsteps of the disease. In the wake of this disaster, a remarkable rebuilding occurred. Within a few years, a series of institutions were launched—schools, orphanages, bookstores, museums, a chemical laboratory, a hospital, bakeries, farms, and various other social enterprises.

At the forefront of this social reconstruction was August Hermann Franke. Moved by the plight of the orphaned children of Glaucha, he set about rebuilding the town. Franke's life had been changed through his involvement in small renewal cells that existed throughout a Lutheran church that had drifted into a spiritual stagnation. Small groups of believers, inspired by Martin Luther's encouragement to begin little churches within the church, began to meet to study the Scriptures, to pray and spur each other in their spiritual lives. Franke noted that before his involvement in this small group,

"My theology I set in my head and not in my heart . . . it was much more a dead science than a living belief."[1]

Franke came to understand through his experience that small groups of committed believers experiencing personal renewal were able to birth or renew churches and institutions, furthering the renewal of culture. German believers, renewed in these "little churches within the church," would inspire many of the key leaders of the revivals that would spread across the world in the following centuries.

THE LITTLE CHURCH WITHIN THE CHURCH

Programs of change and renewal written for businesses, organizations, and governments assume that change will be driven by established leadership. The bible of change management, John P. Kotter's *Leading Change*, recommends the building of a guiding coalition of executives and managers who, through their positional power, can drive an organization toward renewal and effectiveness. Within God's kingdom, however, we are dealing with different dynamics of power.

KEY RENEWAL PRINCIPLE

Renewals emerge from leaders who are positionally weak but spiritually powerful. Revivals burst from groups that are small in number but strong in God's presence.

THE MULTITUDE VS. THE REMNANT

Contemporary corporate models of renewal also assume that change can be driven through PR campaigns, careful image management, and top-down approaches. Such approaches have influenced how we view renewal in the church. The Anglican theologian and pastor Martin Thornton labeled this approach "multitudinism," an approach that attempts to move the multitude simultaneously, and that is naively unaware of the way that God operates and renews His people at different paces.

Reflecting on Thornton's thought, Gerald McDermott writes that the approach of multitudinism "is the theology of the church that is always seeking numbers, more and more people to lasso into the fold. When church leaders are hell-bent on getting more and more warm bodies into the pews, they are wont to relax and hide or even do away with whatever they think might be offputting to the multitudes."[2] A dynamic occurs that parallels what we discovered in the theory of Edwin Friedman in chapter 5—discipleship and spiritual health is reduced to the lowest common denominator in order to move the masses. When this happens, eventually the most spiritually unhealthy and immature set the tone for the congregation, creating a resistance to renewal.

CODEPENDENT PASTORS AND CHURCHES

This can cause a spiritually deadly cycle in which the pastor and church leadership fall into the trap of simply providing an inoffensive, middling, easily digestible spiritual fare, which doesn't create spiritual renewal. Lovelace warns that in such a scenario,

> *Pastors gradually settle down and lose interest in being change agents in the church. An unconscious conspiracy arises between their flesh and that of their congregations. It becomes tacitly understood that the laity will give pastors places of special honour in the exercise of their gifts, if the pastors will agree to leave their congregations' pre-Christian lifestyles undisturbed and do not call for the mobilisation of lay gifts for the work of the kingdom. Pastors are permitted to become ministerial superstars. Their pride is fed and their insecurity is pacified even if they are run ragged, and their congregations are permitted to remain herds of sheep in which each has cheerfully turned to his own way.*[3]

The health of a church is measured by the level of positive feelings experienced. We want renewal, but we also want to please everyone. Thornton noted, however, this is not how God moved in history. He never moves the entire mass of people. Nor does He ensure that everyone is happy. In Scripture we see that God chooses to work with smaller groups—Noah and his family, Abraham and Sarah, Israel among the nations, the faithful remnant within a disobedient Israel and within the church. Gerald McDermott notes that

> we see the same pattern in Jesus' ministry. Why didn't he spend much time with the crowds? Why didn't he go after them when they wandered after getting fed, or when they turned away in repulsion because of his hard sayings? Instead he spent the vast majority of his time with the remnant, the twelve. He went deep with them, and trusted that their inner life, which he cultivated for three years, would radiate. Their lives would attract others.[4]

We see that the way that God shapes and renews us as individuals is remarkably similar to the way He shapes groups of people within the church—remnants—taking them through a process of learning faithfulness in the hidden places, of first shaping them so they can shape others, of creating a ministry within them that emerges from being rather than doing.

KEY RENEWAL PRINCIPLE

This remnant becomes a living and breathing alternative vision, showcasing the spiritual health and vitality that comes when we contend and cry out for God to move.

Thornton, rejecting the approach of multitudinalism, argued for a different approach, seeing three distinct groups within the church:

The Remnant: *Those who are deeply devoted and faithful; their discipleship is at the core of their being. They are not consumers but contenders, carrying the lion's share of the ministry work in a Christian community. They operate not through a sense of duty, but rather genuine Spirit-filled empowerment. Some may be leaders and key influencers within their church; others may have no positional power.*

The Churchgoer: *Those who attend but are living out of a dead orthodoxy, or a faith that is merely a Christian veneer on a thoroughly secular worldview, or cultural Christians, or those who consume rather than contribute wholeheartedly to God's mission within the world. Some of these people may appear to be leaders and stalwarts but are living out of a sense of religious obligation. Thornton compared this group to those who may pay to go watch the football team, but unlike the remnant, they are not on the field, scrapping, tackling, and putting their bodies on the line. These people are the 83% of Christians who a recent survey revealed don't live with a biblical worldview.*[5]

Those Outside the Church: *Deeply loved by God, yet not following Him.*

Thornton's division is similar to the way in which Napoleon described those within his army, known as his "Thirds," in which he noted that a first third of his army would welcome change, the middle third would move as the first third embraced change, and the last third would resist it. By concentrating on the first third, like a worm inching forward, the whole army would progress.[6]

KEY RENEWAL PRINCIPLE

A constant dynamic in the history of the church is
the way in which the larger church is renewed by a
smaller remnant within the church.

The early church was a remnant, filled with the faithful and devoted, its purity reinforced by persecution. However, as it grew, and persecution waned, the problem of cultural Christians and those adhering to faith without full faithfulness emerged. Smaller communities of the faithful remnant have been a constant engine of renewal within the church.

CELLS OF RENEWAL

Martin Luther called these cells of renewal, the little church within the church.[7] This is the origin of the small group structure that is central to so many churches today. When Luther's own movement went into decline, it was Lutherans seeking renewal who met in "colleges of piety," in which the faithful were able to meet for mutual encouragement and the deepening of faith.

The early renewal movements such as the Moravians and the Methodists centered their dynamic growth and missional effectiveness on an interplay between larger church structures and smaller groups dedicated to discipleship and growth. Such places provided a training in discipleship and an environment to live out sanctification in a way that was not possible in larger worship services and church structures.

Returning to our renewal cycle, as individuals experience renewal—moving through confession and repentance, taking up the posture of contention, being formed around patterns of formation, discipleship, and influence, and gathering with others to encourage each other in these goals—a remnant is formed. This is a key element of the renewal cycle.

> The taking up of renewal patterns, the adoption of a contending posture, the seeking of the presence, all come together to offer a renewed purpose for the church, which is embodied by the remnant.

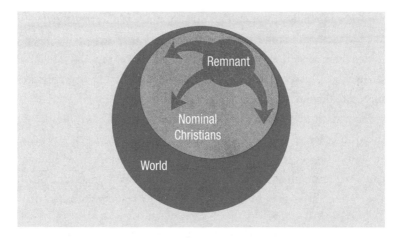

The remnant models the life of Jesus, who vicariously served the whole, by living a sacrificial, prophetic life. The remnant serves the broader church and culture by living sacrificially the faithful and prophetic life.

Thornton saw the remnant as the pumping heart, which sent life-giving blood into the rest of the system. Remnants are physically in proximity to others, but in worship, they are at a distance, defined and shaped around the wholehearted devotion of God with the whole of their lives. It is this difference that enables God to use them to serve others.

Remnants serve the broader culture by disobeying its patterns of worship while contending for its renewal.

REMNANTS MUST BE BAPTIZED IN RENEWAL TO AVOID SCHISMATIC PRIDE

While such groups have brought renewal and even revival to the church, they also can easily flip, becoming schismatic and divisive. Renewal movements often pick up on a long-ignored or forgotten element of theology or practice, and God may use this neglected element as part of the renewal. However, when the neglected factor becomes the main thing, instead of part of the larger tapestry of God's renewal, a divisive spirit of pride, division, and fleshly attitudes can enter into the renewing remnant.

This spiritual pride replaces the presence as the gathering point. Soon impatience overrides contending. Human power creeps back in. A holy discontent and hunger for God to move among a younger renewing remnant can easily be subverted by the flesh and the devil into a generational conflict, which leads to fragmentation rather than renewal.

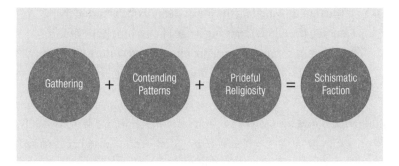

The remnant leaves the system, no longer becoming a renewal cell but instead is now merely another schismatic faction. Sadly, in other circumstances, because of the pure toxicity of the system and its descent into an irretrievable heresy or departure from biblical faith, the renewal cell must, for the sake of its own health, with a heavy and humble heart, break away for a new growth to begin in healthier soil.

The presence should always lead us to humility, to a desire to serve rather than split.

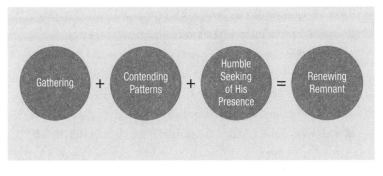

REMNANTS HAVE SKIN IN THE RENEWAL

A remnant's ability to be a cell of renewal flows from its living out of the renewal. It becomes a miniature revival, a place to live out a renewal life while we wait on God to pour out His Spirit with power on the wider church and culture.

> Remnants have skin in the renewal. They risk everything on His goodness, which turns out to be no risk at all. For the ultimate risk is not to risk it all upon renewal.

Remnants are not communities built around opinion or critique. Instead, they enflesh the presence-driven renewal. In our age of opinion, social media venting, virtue signaling, and image management, remnants choose a different path, to pursue, with others, in the hidden places, the eternal perspective, to cry and contend, to step into the gap. Choosing not punditry but contention. Instead, their way is prayer. Central to renewal cells and remnants in every move of God is the practice of contending prayer.

REMNANTS ARE HOT HOUSES OF CONTENDING PRAYER

Observing the secularism that was emerging at the midpoint of the twentieth century, Martyn Lloyd-Jones saw that the challenge facing the church in the West was unlike anything that had been encountered before.

I see a very great difference between today and two hundred years ago, or indeed even one hundred years ago. The difficulty in those early times was that men and women were in a state of apathy. They were more or less asleep. Going back, certainly two hundred years, there was no eternal denial of Christian truth. It was just that people did not trouble to practice it. They more or less assumed it. And in a sense, all you had to do was awaken them and to rouse them, and to disturb them out of their lethargy.[8]

Yet now, Jones warned, "the kind of problem facing us is altogether deeper and more desperate than that which has confronted the Christian church for many a long century."[9] The emerging secularism and post-Christian society confronting Jones in 1959 has only grown in strength and power in the resulting decades. The problems are now even more mountainous. Jones warned his fellow Christians that the temptation to treat this challenge with the silver bullets of more effective methods, better programming, or slicker use of technology would do nothing to halt this lumbering juggernaut.

Using the story of Jesus and the possessed boy in Mark's gospel, Jones compared the church of his day to the disciples who had had success casting out spirits in the name of Jesus; however, encountering a powerful demon possessing a boy, they failed to deliver the child. Returning to Jesus bemused, they enquired of their failing, to which Jesus replied that this kind of powerful demon only comes out by prayer and fasting. Jones saw the church of his day attempting to exorcize the demon of post-Christianity in the manner that had worked in the past. Yet this stronghold of secularism was more powerful. "We must cease to have so much confidence in ourselves, and in all our methods and organisations, and in all our slickness."[10] For this kind would only come out with prayer and fasting, in a desperate and hungry turning to God.

I shall see no hope until individual members of the Church are praying for revival, perhaps meeting in one another's homes, meeting in groups amongst friends, meeting together in churches, meeting anywhere you like, and praying with urgency and concentration for a shedding forth of the power of God, such as he shed forth one hundred and two hundred years ago, and in every other period of revival, and of reawakening. There is no hope until we do. But the moment we do, hope enters.[11]

Those renewed, experiencing a microcosm of revival within themselves, those who are hungry and thirsting for righteousness, find each other. We discover that much of our holy discontent is born of a life that is suffering from what Richard Foster calls "the agony of prayerlessness."[12] Our lives are designed to be in intimate relationship and friendship with God. When we don't pray, we become spiritually dehydrated. Understanding now that the challenges of life are to be met not with futile human striving but on the bended knee, prayer becomes indispensable to living.

As we step into contending prayer, no longer do we fill awkward silence with perfunctory prayers and laundry lists of inconsequential requests. Instead, rumbling, reverberating, desperate prayers begin.

Prayer begins: *Eventually holy discontent forms into a desire to pray that can no longer be ignored. With the status quo no longer tolerated, the only way forward is to cry out to God for His intervention into the world. Prayer moves from something desirable but rarely practiced in the Christian life to something indispensable and foundational.*

Small groups begin praying: *A handful of people find each other. They are united by their driving desire to pray and contend for God to act. In the north of Scotland, two elderly disabled sisters prayed together by their fire, leading to the Hebridean revival. The revival that broke out in*

*New York during the nineteenth century can be traced back to a hand-
ful of businessmen praying at lunch in a small room in Wall Street. The
awakening that occurred in South India in the 1930s was contended for
by three preteen boys, who had become transformed by God, and early
each morning prayed in the jungle on the edges of their town.*

Contending and standing in the gap: *Prayer that proceeds God moving is
contending prayer. To contend is to struggle, to stretch for something.
This is proactive prayer, beseeching God to move, in which we cry out
for God's mercy on behalf of ourselves, our communities, and nations.
To, as the book of Ezekiel states, "Stand before me in the gap on behalf of
the land" (22:30).*

Contending prayer is spiritual warfare: *As we adopt the posture of contending, it becomes vital to understand that we are not contending
against those who come against us in opposition, but as Scripture
teaches us, the powers and principalities, the forces that resist Christ's
rule, wishing to keep us in a state of enslavement, and oppose God's
plan of renewal in the world. We practice contending prayer, then, to
acknowledge that God fights our spiritual battles for us.*

KEY RENEWAL PRINCIPLE
Renewal only comes with prayer and fasting.

Contending prayer then becomes normative amongst those seeking renewal. Such prayer asks God to change our churches, our culture, and our world, yet it also changes us as we pray, reshaping us in
the patterns of the kingdom.

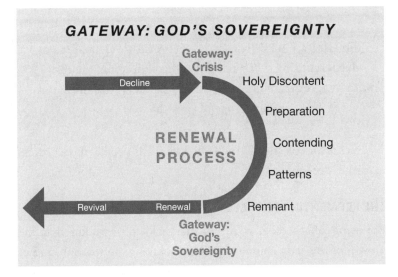

WE CANNOT MAKE REVIVAL HAPPEN

In our renewal cycle, we reach another transition gateway. We can move from holy discontent to confession and repentance, we can move from consuming to a posture of contending for renewal. We can gather around forming patterns, solidifying into a remnant, a cell contending for renewal. But can we call for God to break out revival? The wide-scale pouring out of His Spirit, in which churches, movements, regions, cities, countries, and continents are changed? We can desire, hope for, cry out for such a move, but we cannot make it happen. Only God can cause such a mighty move of His Spirit. But we can contend and wait.

Strategies of renewal, which attempt to make revival happen on our terms and timetable, fall back into the error of religiosity, trying to run ahead of God and force His hand through the power of human striving. Such errors, rightly intended, wrongly create kinds of Babelic revival structures, falling into the temptation of using the dynamics of hype, manipulation, and image management. As with all religiosity, exhaustion arrives quickly, with disillusionment soon to follow.

> **KEY RENEWAL PRINCIPLE**
>
> Sometimes, God will delay revival breakthrough to send us deeper into His will. For if breakthrough comes too early, with its accompanying fruit, we may not be spiritually mature enough to tend God's harvest.

To care for His crop, He will often send His people into a process of further deepening.

THE FERMENTING PROCESS

Bouncing off theologian Alfred Harnack's observation that the growth of the early church was like a bubbling, mysterious kind of fermenting process, Alan Kreider writes of the process of the early church,

> *The ferment was happening. It was brewing, but not under anyone's control. It was uncoordinated, it was unpredictable, and it seemed unstoppable. The ferment was spontaneous, and it involved ordinary ingredients that at times synergized into a heady brew. The churches grew in many places. . . . They proliferated because the faith that these fishers and hunters embodied was attractive to people who were dissatisfied with their old cultural and religious habits, who felt pushed to explore new possibilities, and who then encountered Christians who embodied a new manner of life that pulled them toward what the Christians called "rebirth" into a new life.*[13]

When we patiently wait, contending for God to move, our efforts are not in vain. The longer we patiently and faithfully contend, a process akin to fermentation takes place. Just think of the cucumber that turns into a pickle. The cucumber undergoes a process of being set aside, hidden away in the dark, immersed in salt. It is broken down, yet it does not spoil. Instead, this process releases healthy bacteria, the kind of which scientists have discovered is essential for the health of our guts, and our entire systems. The method of breaking down transforms the cucumber, releasing something in it powerfully healing, useful for releasing health into systems. The longer the cucumber is set apart in the process of being broken down, the more powerful the fermentation.

> The longer a remnant remains contending—
> moving deeper into God's process of sanctification,
> set apart in hiddenness—the lengthier the crying out for
> His presence, the more powerful the fermentation.

A healthy bacteria is produced in them and is released into the system. God controls when revival breaks out; all we can do is step into His process of growth. Often, He allows the process of fermentation to occur for decades until renewal bursts outward.

Chapter 13

When Renewal Goes Viral

How Form and Fire Empower Revival

Violently taken from his home by slave traders, Patrick found himself forced to work outdoors, exiled from his home and his people. Alienated, enslaved, and miserably cold, Patrick found a fire of faith warming him from the inside. As he tended the flocks of his captors, in the midst of isolation and crisis, God came close and real. John O'Donohue writes, "Patrick is able to survive these harsh and lonely territories of exile precisely because he keeps the beauty of God alive in his heart. The inner beauty of the divine intimacy transfigures the outer bleakness. This inner intimacy brings his soul alive. It opens the world of the divine imagination to this youth. Consequently, he becomes available for his destiny in a new way."[1]

Led by a series of visions, Patrick escaped his captors, returning home to Britain. He began training in the ministry, and possibly trained with Martin of Tours. A remnant of believers began to coalesce around him. One night in a dream, Patrick saw a vision of his former captors, who cried out to him, begging him to return and walk the ways of God among them. Inspired, Patrick returned to Ireland around AD 432. With him is his remnant, who now operate as an apostolic band. Skilfully and courageously, Patrick and his band communicate and exemplify the gospel among the Irish tribes in innovative, cultural ways in which they can understand. A remarkable move of God occurs—thousands are saved, vast numbers of churches planted, priests and leaders trained. The face of the land is profoundly altered. Louis Gougand writes of Patrick's legacy,

> Most certainly he did not succeed in converting all the heathens of the island; but he won so many of them for Christ, he founded so many churches, ordained so many clerics, kindled such a zeal in men's hearts, that it seems right to believe that to him was directly due the wonderful blossoming of Christianity which distinguished Ireland in the following ages.[2]

Patrick had experienced the full gamut of renewal. The personal renewal that had occurred during his captivity in Ireland now overflowed into a full-blown nationwide revival.

RENEWAL BEGINS TO BREAK OUT

Revival occurs when the time of fermenting is over and God in His grace comes close. A new move of God happens as renewal goes viral. An incredibly exciting moment occurs—the remnant becomes a majority within a church. Renewal breaks out into other systems—churches, movements, and cultures.

> **KEY RENEWAL PRINCIPLE**
> Revival is renewal gone viral.

RENEWAL SPREADS TO CHURCHES AND CONGREGATIONS

The church becomes what Mike Breen in his exploration of the book of Acts called a hot center. He writes of the red-hot center that the church in Jerusalem was in Acts 5:12–16:

> *The gravitational pull of this red-hot center was so strong that, even though everyone did his or her best not to be around these people, they couldn't. They kept coming. That is how strong the gravitational field was. More people became disciples. More people were healed. More people were delivered.*[3]

Churches with such vitality inevitably give birth, spawning plants, congregations, missionaries, sent leaders, and inspirited imitators. The renewal fills our spiritual systems with bursting life that sprays out into the world.

Such churches act as apostolic hubs, bases of renewal, spreading presence-filled believers out into the world.

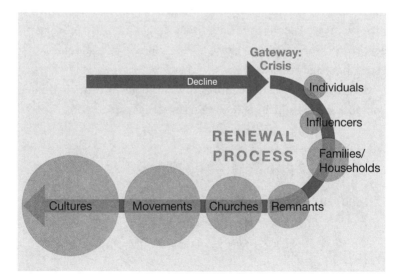

RENEWAL REVIVES AND CREATES MOVEMENTS

Just as the nonanxious agent of renewal brings health to a social system, and precisely as the faithful remnant brings life to a church, now the church acts as a healing agent within systems. These may be church networks, denominations, or geographical regions. The health begins to spread. Sure, there are setbacks, counterattacks of the enemy, human failings, and misunderstandings, yet God's kingdom is advanced. Ground is taken.

He continues as He has throughout history to move history toward His ends. The renewal movement is filled with His presence and becomes a vehicle He uses to connect people with His glory. These renewal movements become containers and distributors of the move of God, as lines of relationship and influence grow between people and places touched by God's renewing hand.

CULTURES

Situated as we are in the world, every element of this system is connected to the cultures outside of the church. At crucial points in history, we see such movements connecting with other movements across the world, spilling out into the culture in profound ways, changing society in radical ways.

During these powerful moves of God, often with their unique contours, we can still observe several key elements.

PRESENCE COMES WITH POWER

LOUD AND QUIET: *When His presence comes with power to revive us, be it a personal renewal or a large-scale awakening, change occurs at deep levels. Sometimes this occurs in powerful ways, His presence causing people to cry out in conviction during services or display un-*

usual effects of the Spirit's visitation. Other renewals are quieter, less obvious, but profoundly change those they touch at the core of their being, the presence moving them to greater levels of Christlikeness.

ENCOUNTER WITH HIS PRESENCE: When His presence comes with power, reordering much of human life. Being in His presence becomes the most important thing. Whereas prayer and worship may have been like chores before, now we can sit in His presence for hours. Our priorities are reordered, the world looks different, everything is brought into an eternal perspective. Our individual and corporate lives are drawn into His.

EMPOWERED AND QUICKENED

FROM STRIVING TO EMPOWERED: God's presence draws close to empower His mission in the world and to reconnect us with our original purpose of spreading His glory to the ends of the earth. When renewal comes, we are empowered in that mission. The years of struggling in our own strength to complete His mission are replaced by a quickening as He becomes our primary power source. As Stuart Piggin writes, the drawing near of the Holy Spirit in renewal is "to give those gifts which promote the gospel by glorifying Jesus and his kingdom and which empower Christians for the work of evangelism and mission."[4]

MINISTRY IS EMPOWERED: With His Spirit rather than the flesh now empowering our ministry, a holy weight now pervades our preaching, our evangelism, our teaching, our serving the poor. Breakthroughs become a regular business. What before was a struggle to break up the dirt to plant kingdom seeds now becomes the harvesting of fruit.

GROWTH, ADVANCE, AND FRUIT

PERSONAL AND CORPORATE TRANSFORMATION: *The fruit of the harvest is the transformation of individual lives, communities, cultures, and nations. A beachhead is taken in enemy territory. The strongholds of the enemy are broken, kingdom fruit becomes normal as individual lives, communities, and cultures begin to display the will of God. The work of God advances forward with power.*

INFLUENCED AND INFLUENTIAL

We have discovered the way in which we live and exist in systems that are interconnected. It is the same for the church and the world. The church is a network of individuals, leaders and influencers, micro-communities, remnants, congregations, movements, and denominations. All of these systems exist, live, and serve within cultures, which in turn are interconnected in a globalized world. As we continue to examine our world through a systemic lens, another key insight is revealed to us.

> Those positioned to have significant influence are most likely to themselves be influenced.

Go anywhere in the world, and you will find Chinese people starting businesses, creating culture, and trading. The influence of Chinese culture on the planet is immense. Most Chinese influencers who have gone out into the world can personally, or through family ties, trace their origins back to the port cities and regions of southern China, regions whose location gives them strategic influence in the world. Yet this positioning of influence also means that these areas are the most susceptible to influence themselves. Throughout history, the port cities and regions of southern China are where outside ideas, political ideologies, foreign religions, and illicit trades have entered the country. At points, these ports were even occupied by foreign forces. Port regions are nodes interconnected to a more extensive system, bringing opportunities such as trade and cultural influence, yet also connecting China to outside contagions that it wished to avoid. This illustrates a key insight when it comes to influence and renewal in a globalized, connected world.

INFLUENTIAL AND INFLUENCED

The more you are positioned to influence, the more you will be susceptible to be affected. This is an increasing reality in our hyperconnected and globalized world. This is as true now for individuals as it is for churches and nations. The ability of the world to influence and shape our inner worlds through new technologies and the techniques of public relations is unprecedented. In the face of such developments, fearing a routing of the church in the face of such soft power, there is growing advocacy of a kind of strategic retreat, for Christians to withdraw from places of influence to avoid being influenced. There is a good argument for withdrawing from particularly unhelpful strategies of Christian influence that rely on human rather than divine effort. A religious retreat, however, in our increasingly interconnected world, becomes increasingly impossible.

> In our hyperconnected world, a Christian strategy
> of retreat is impossible.

EVERYTHING IS NOW CLOSE

Past generations of Christians could retreat from the moral corruption of surrounding societies by withdrawing geographically. As their society collapsed into corruption and sin, the Christians of the third century, known as the Desert Fathers and Mothers, could flee to the uncontaminated Egyptian wilderness. Yet such a change of location will today not have the same effect. Philosopher Anthony Giddens notes that the contemporary world is marked by a collapsing of time and space, in which a retreat to another location cannot prevent influence by outside forces.

Giddens writes that now, "Locales are thoroughly penetrated by and shaped in terms of social influences quite distant from them."[5] We are still influenced and formed by what is visible and local, yet also what is distant shapes us powerfully. Giddens observes that influences that are distant are now strangely continually present.

Religious groups that seek to escape the contemporary world will still find its influences present and powerful, in ways unknown in the past. The religious sociologist Peter L. Berger notes that while the Orthodox Jew may live within a community that distances itself from the world through retreating and living within a cultural and religious enclave, yet "all that individual has to do to get out of his alleged Jewish destiny is to walk out and take the subway. Outside, waiting, is the emporium of life-styles, identities, and religious preferences."[6]

You can physically remove yourself, yet mentally, emotionally, and spiritually still be shaped by distant forces. Mission and ministry strategies that nobly attempt to live and minister locally, embedding themselves in the web of neighborhood relationships, will still find the "distant" forces of globalization present, shaping both their communities and their personal lives.

> We live in the space between relationships and communities that are physically close and a hyperconnected world of distant yet present influences.

Contemporary life is lived in the overlap between influences and relationships that are physically close, and our hyperconnectivity that connects us to influences and relationships that are distant yet powerfully present due to technology. As we have learned, this means we can be easily influenced. Yet it also means that we can be influential.

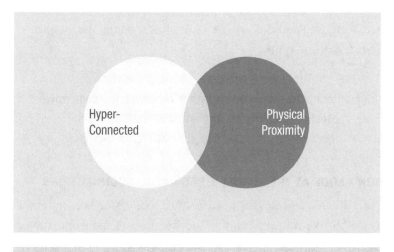

KEY RENEWAL PRINCIPLE
Throughout history, at moments where the world
has become interconnected through human
infrastructure, God has initiated renewals.

HIJACKING THE INFRASTRUCTURE OF EMPIRE FOR THE KINGDOM OF GOD

The journey of the gospel out from the upper room to the ends of the Empire was lubricated by the Roman road and the *Cursus Publicus*—the imperial mail system. The Roman Empire was a technologically connected world, offering both a threat to the nascent church through its hard and soft power, but also an opportunity to have its own infrastructure hijacked by the kingdom of God. As this Roman infrastructure fell into ruin during the Middle Ages and resurgent paganism pushed Christianity to the icy peripheries of Europe, the

Celtic Christians of Ireland simply went lo-fi, setting to sea in fragile boats, allowing the primal sea currents to send them where God and the waves led. The silk roads carrying trade and gold, connecting East and West, would also become a vein of faith, taking the message of Christ deep into China.

> The world is a system—it always has been, connected by trade and migration. Now, with the connective tissue of technology bringing the world close, the possibilities of global Christian influence increase.

DON'T LOOK AT THE BORDERS; LOOK AT THE CONNECTIONS

Parag Khanna encourages us to not just look at the borders of the world but the connections, for "the true map of the world should feature not just states but megacities, highways, railways, pipelines, Internet cables, and other symbols of our emerging global network civilization."[7] All created for human advancement, yet also ways in which God is moving history toward His ends by bringing us closer, creating possibilities for His project to partner with humans in the spread of His presence to the ends of the world.

The failing renewal of secularism promises us a global utopia, created by human hands. Yet as globalization brings the world closer, it seems we are being drawn apart as tribalism and cultural conflict seem to increase. At the same time, the hyperconnective technology that brings us closer contributes to the social atomization and loneliness that we experience, pushing us further away from those to whom we live in physical proximity. In the eighteenth and nineteenth centuries, modernity, the Industrial Revolution, and globalization created a global society, yet also increased social fracturing, injustice, and cultural upheaval. Into this space, God refashioned the church through a series of powerful revivals. The old frameworks of parish boundaries became irrelevant as a culture of movement and migration began. The emerging individualism of early modernity wrought significant damage to religious structures built during feudal times. Established churches struggled to minister to and provide for individuals and communities shaped by this new cultural reality.

The new move of God saw individuals themselves transformed by the gospel and animated by His presence, engaged in mission and ministry on the frontiers of this globalizing and emerging modernity. Into the social isolation created by the tectonic shifts in society, those shaped by the renewal created a whole new social universe of Christian "civil societies," from Methodist groups devoted to pure discipleship, to groups coming together to show God's love to abused animals or to those suffering from the scourge of slavery.

While this moment was theologically orthodox, church historian Mark A. Noll writes that "because its spirituality was adjusted to an opening world of commerce, communications and empire, that spirituality effectively resolved the psychological dilemmas created by this opening world."[8] Our current moment is an extension and intensification of the globalizing modernity that was dawning in the eighteenth and nineteenth centuries, which logically is creating similar social and psychological dilemmas but with higher intensity. Are we adjusting to meet these challenges? Are we punch drunk by the problems of our age, or do we see the opportunities before us? Do we sense the possibilities of embodied and enfleshed Christian community in a time of disembodied isolation? In a time of anxiety and mental exhaustion, are we seeing the rich traditions of prayer, contemplation, and meditation upon God as antidotes to our exhausted brains? In a time of social fracturing and cultural polarization, do we understand the powerful place that exists at the communion table? These are a few examples, but there are countless opportunities to be discovered. We are only limited by our own imaginations, a problem

God Himself does not have. Let us listen to the fertile fields of creative solutions that He wishes us to walk into.

> ## We need a great awakening where Christians are influential without being influenced.

Yet how does this happen, and how can it happen with the particular challenges and opportunities of our time?

FORMATIONAL AND WORSHIPING DISTANCE

The people of God, both in the Hebrew Scriptures and the New Testament, found themselves living in proximity to those who did not worship God, and they were thus vulnerable to being formed and shaped by the ideas and the idols of paganism. They also found themselves in a world of empires and surrounding nations, linking and connecting the ancient world of the Levant, bringing distant thoughts, cultures, and gods close.

The Roman Empire brought even more distant influences and more formational power into the life of the early church. The church was called to be in the world but not of it. This meant being connected, living in physical proximity, using the infrastructure of connection, but keeping a worshiping and formational distance. They were to worship the one true God, and they were to be formed by Him.

> ## They were to be physically close to their neighbors, yet their minds and lives were to be set upon and shaped by heaven.

While physically close to their neighbors and the influences around them, the early church had key distances:

FORMATIONAL DISTANCE: Being physically close to others and present in a dominant culture, while being formed by a different set of influences, practices, and relationships.

WORSHIPING DISTANCE: Being physically close to others and present in a dominant culture, while worshiping and being empowered by a different divine source of power.

The church and followers of Jesus are called to be human temples. Temples are built around form and fire. Their forms direct our patterns of worship and our hearts toward God, reshaping true worshipers in God's image. Temples are also places of fire, where fire is used to consume sacrifices, cleansing and purifying us. In Scripture, fire also symbolizes God's presence and power.

For ancient Israel, the temple, when functioning as God intended it, enabled Israel to be close to her neighbors but gave them formational distance. It also gave them worshiping distance as they centered their lives around God's purifying, empowering presence.

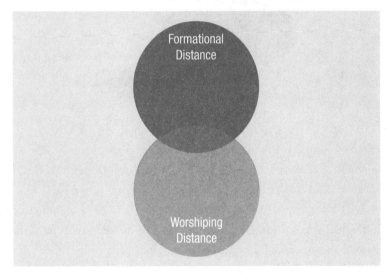

FORM AND FIRE

As we learned in chapter 8, we are human temples, the church is a temple of the Holy Spirit, and Jesus is also now the temple. His way is the form, His presence and Spirit is the fire. Healthy biblical renewal is like a bird with two wings—form and fire. We need His fire to come, His empowering presence, to do what human strength cannot. We need His fire to come to cleanse us and purify us, accelerate our ministry and mission. We need His fire to smash strongholds, and to take spiritual ground for the kingdom. Yet we also need His form to shape us. We need holy patterns to remake us in Christlikeness.

THE TWO WINGS OF RENEWAL

Form

Fire

Many Christian traditions are strong on forms; others are all about chasing fire. In the face of the secularist challenge, a whole new generation of young Christians is seeking a breakthrough in God's presence and power, through passionate worship, prayer, and mission. Others, aware of the corrosive influence of our contemporary individualism, are integrating and pursuing the patterns that have shaped and sustained the church for millennia. However, those pursuing fire without form—in a culture obsessed with the spectacular, feelings, and the instantaneous—can find themselves being carried away with sheer human enthusiasm or disillusioned when God's timetable doesn't align with theirs.

Those committed to formational patterns overtime may find such forms beneficial for individual shaping, yet impotent for kingdom breakthrough. The patterns can become emptied of their meaning, forms without fire, giving into a theology and faith of drudgery and defeat.

Tim Keller, while affirming the revitalization that revivalism has brought to the church of the West, notes that it needs forms that guide us into consistent discipleship. At a time when most Christians were caught in cultural Christianity and dead orthodoxy, revivalism rightly re-emphasized the importance of our individual relationship with God, of our hearts being changed by the Holy Spirit. However, Keller notes that this emphasis of revivalism also has contributed to contemporary forms of Christianity found across the West where individuals seek out the fire of individual experience but shun the formational practices of the gathered Christian church. Keller advocates for what he calls "ecclesial revivalism,"[9] in which the energy of revivalism moves us into the formational context of the church. This is form and fire, a pursuing of His presence, the release of divine empowering, alongside patterns that form us into renewed vessels of that presence.

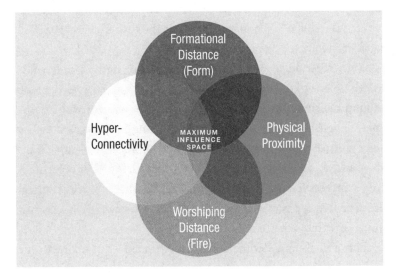

The twenty-first century has placed the church in the West in a hyperconnected world increasingly experiencing the reality of its flight from God. If we can be a church of fire and form, influential for the kingdom rather than influenced by the world, then we will we find ourselves presented with a phenomenal opportunity. One that should not be met with dismay but anticipation and excitement. The real question is: Are you ready?

DO IT AGAIN, LORD

It's a sunny June day in London, and five of us are squashed into a tiny upstairs room. After sensing that God wanted us to visit historic sites of revival to pray for renewal, my wife, Trudi, and I have flown twenty-five hours across the world. We are in a small prayer room attached to John Wesley's bedroom, now converted into a museum. Here, each morning, on bended knee, Wesley would open his Bible and pray. It occurs to me that this room was the furnace of prayer, which drove much of the revival that spread out across the world in the eighteenth century. I think of the small stone Wesleyan chapel, a couple of miles from our house, built by Methodist missionaries, who would travel out of Melbourne, preaching the gospel on horseback, in what must have felt like another planet.

My tourist demeanor is punctuated as the Nigerian tour guide kneels down at Wesley's bench and asks me to pray. Surprised, I look around the small room. Next to me is a Korean pastor who doesn't speak English and his friend who is wearing a fluorescent yellow shirt with "Revival" written across the front. My wife glances at his shirt and smiles at me. I begin to pray, tempted to offer a perfunctory and reserved prayer, but then it hits me where we are standing. This room, this city, out of which God burst a renewal beyond parish boundaries into the world.

For well over a decade I have interpreted and recorded our

post-Christian moment, all while pastoring in the grit and grind of secular soil. I think of the friends and colleagues who are no longer in ministry, those who had walked away from faith, the churches I knew that had shut their doors, the mission movements that were on their last legs. Dare I hope that God will again pour out His power on us?

I can't even remember what I prayed first, but I think it was a prayer of thanks for Wesley. But this moment wasn't about praying a mere nod to what had gone before. Here the past was an inspiration, a dangerous counternarrative to our myth of inevitable decline. Another story to remind us that in a secularizing moment of globalization, God can still move. So, my prayer shifted to the future.

"God, do it again."

"God, revive us again."

"Raise another generation of John Wesleys."

Trudi raises her hands in praise; soon the Koreans are praying as only Koreans pray. As English and Korean prayers fill the air, a museum again becomes a place of worship. A sacred space is carved out. My heart fills. The defeat that has lingered over me for fifteen years disappears. A disappointment so assumed that I didn't notice I was wearing it like a shirt.

Wesley's great achievement was not that he sang his own song, but that he rediscovered God's song, and sang it afresh over a newly emerging landscape.[10] That is the heart of renewal. The soundtrack of revival. That is what we are being called to do again. Will you sing God's song over our secularized Western culture, over our globalized world? Will you contend? Will you seek out the hungry and form a remnant? Will you seek His presence with all your heart? Will you, with a growing chorus of millions across our world, cry out, "Do it again, Lord"?

Weekly Group Framework— Building a Remnant

GROUP SCHEDULE: 1 HOUR

10 minutes – Prayer, worship, and Scripture.

10 minutes – Spin the pen to see who will share a compelling summary of the chapter. If it lands on the same person two weeks in a row, that is just how the cookie crumbles, keeping all group members in a position of readiness to learn.

15 minutes – Group discusses what principle impacted them from this week's reading.

10 minutes – Group explains how they integrated last week's learning, and how this week's learning will be integrated into action and practice during the week.

15 minutes – Contending prayer for God to bring renewal in your personal lives, your church, your neighborhood, your town or city, your school or workplace, your nation, and the world.

BEGIN WITH WORSHIP – Sing, read a psalm, praise God for what He has done in your lives. Whatever you choose to do, begin by glorifying God. Make this time about Him.

SPIN THE PEN – The person who the pen points to shares their summary of the chapter using the five points below that they prepared earlier as they read the chapter.

CHAPTER I: THE SECULARIST RENEWAL MYTH
Presence and Progress on the Road to Renewal

WHAT KEY THINGS DID I LEARN FROM THIS CHAPTER?

1. _____

_____

_____

_____

_____

2. _____

_____

_____

_____

_____

3. _____

_____

_____

_____

_____

4. _____

_____

_____

_____

_____

5. _____

_____

_____

_____

_____

REFLECTIONS AND GROUP LEARNING – Discuss as a group.

What is one renewal principle that you learned in this week's reading? Each person shares one principle that has been discovered.

_____

_____

_____

_____

PARTNERING WITH GOD IN RENEWAL

Share how you each went about integrating last week's chapter into your life and practice. After reflecting on this chapter, what is one personal change you will make this week to partner with God in His plan of renewal? Share with the group, which will keep each other accountable next week.

_____

_____

_____

_____

_____

_____

_____

CONTEND IN PRAYER

What is God asking you to cry out and contend for this week? Contend in prayer for renewal together.

CHAPTER 2: THE RENEWAL PATTERN
From Holy Discontent to Corporate Revival

WHAT KEY THINGS DID I LEARN FROM THIS CHAPTER?

1. _____

_____

_____

_____

_____

2. _____

_____

_____

_____

_____

3. _____

_____

_____

_____

_____

4. _____

_____

_____

_____

_____

5. _____

_____

_____

_____

REFLECTIONS AND GROUP LEARNING – Discuss as a group.

What is one renewal principle that you learned in this week's reading? Each person shares one principle that has been discovered.

_____

_____

_____

_____

PARTNERING WITH GOD IN RENEWAL

Share how you each went about integrating last week's chapter into your life and practice. After reflecting on this chapter, what is one personal change you will make this week to partner with God in His plan of renewal? Share with the group, which will keep each other accountable next week.

_____

_____

_____

_____

_____

_____

_____

CONTEND IN PRAYER

What is God asking you to cry out and contend for this week? Contend in prayer for renewal together.

CHAPTER 3: CRISIS: THE GATEWAY TO RENEWAL
The Silver Lining to Be Found in Dark Clouds

WHAT KEY THINGS DID I LEARN FROM THIS CHAPTER?

1. _____
_____
_____
_____
_____

2. _____
_____
_____
_____
_____

3. _____
_____
_____
_____
_____

4. _____
_____
_____
_____
_____

5. _____
_____
_____
_____
_____

REFLECTIONS AND GROUP LEARNING – Discuss as a group.
What is one renewal principle that you learned in this week's reading? Each person shares one principle that has been discovered.

_____

_____

_____

_____

PARTNERING WITH GOD IN RENEWAL
Share how you each went about integrating last week's chapter into your life and practice. After reflecting on this chapter, what is one personal change you will make this week to partner with God in His plan of renewal? Share with the group, which will keep each other accountable next week.

_____

_____

_____

_____

_____

_____

_____

CONTEND IN PRAYER
What is God asking you to cry out and contend for this week? Contend in prayer for renewal together.

CHAPTER 4: FROM DISSATISFACTION TO HOLY DISCONTENT
Ripe for Renewal in the Ruin of Meaninglessness and Unlimited Freedom

WHAT KEY THINGS DID I LEARN FROM THIS CHAPTER?

1. _____

_____

_____

_____

_____

2. _____

_____

_____

_____

_____

3. _____

_____

_____

_____

_____

4. _____

_____

_____

_____

_____

5. _____

_____

_____

_____

_____

REFLECTIONS AND GROUP LEARNING – Discuss as a group.

What is one renewal principle that you learned in this week's reading? Each person shares one principle that has been discovered.

_____

_____

_____

_____

PARTNERING WITH GOD IN RENEWAL

Share how you each went about integrating last week's chapter into your life and practice. After reflecting on this chapter, what is one personal change you will make this week to partner with God in His plan of renewal? Share with the group, which will keep each other accountable next week.

_____

_____

_____

_____

_____

_____

_____

CONTEND IN PRAYER

What is God asking you to cry out and contend for this week? Contend in prayer for renewal together.

CHAPTER 5: RENEWAL IN AN ANXIOUS CULTURE
Fostering Peaceful Presence in the Age of Outrage and Radical Individualism

WHAT KEY THINGS DID I LEARN FROM THIS CHAPTER?

1. _____

_____

_____

_____

_____

2. _____

_____

_____

_____

_____

3. _____

_____

_____

_____

_____

4. _____

_____

_____

_____

_____

5. _____

_____

_____

_____

_____

REFLECTIONS AND GROUP LEARNING – Discuss as a group.

What is one renewal principle that you learned in this week's reading? Each person shares one principle that has been discovered.

_____

_____

_____

_____

PARTNERING WITH GOD IN RENEWAL

Share how you each went about integrating last week's chapter into your life and practice. After reflecting on this chapter, what is one personal change you will make this week to partner with God in His plan of renewal? Share with the group, which will keep each other accountable next week.

_____

_____

_____

_____

_____

_____

_____

CONTEND IN PRAYER

What is God asking you to cry out and contend for this week? Contend in prayer for renewal together.

CHAPTER 6: SECULARISM VS. THE PRESENCE
From Temples of Exhaustion to Temples of Presence

WHAT KEY THINGS DID I LEARN FROM THIS CHAPTER?

1. _____

_____

_____

_____

_____

2. _____

_____

_____

_____

_____

3. _____

_____

_____

_____

_____

4. _____

_____

_____

_____

_____

5. _____

_____

_____

_____

_____

REFLECTIONS AND GROUP LEARNING – Discuss as a group.

What is one renewal principle that you learned in this week's reading? Each person shares one principle that has been discovered.

_____

_____

_____

_____

PARTNERING WITH GOD IN RENEWAL

Share how you each went about integrating last week's chapter into your life and practice. After reflecting on this chapter, what is one personal change you will make this week to partner with God in His plan of renewal? Share with the group, which will keep each other accountable next week.

_____

_____

_____

_____

_____

_____

_____

CONTEND IN PRAYER

What is God asking you to cry out and contend for this week? Contend in prayer for renewal together.

CHAPTER 7: RENEWAL TO THE ENDS OF THE EARTH
God's Plan to Fill the Cosmos with His Presence

WHAT KEY THINGS DID I LEARN FROM THIS CHAPTER?

1. _____

_____

_____

_____

_____

2. _____

_____

_____

_____

_____

3. _____

_____

_____

_____

_____

4. _____

_____

_____

_____

_____

5. _____

_____

_____

_____

REFLECTIONS AND GROUP LEARNING – Discuss as a group.

What is one renewal principle that you learned in this week's reading? Each person shares one principle that has been discovered.

_____

_____

_____

_____

PARTNERING WITH GOD IN RENEWAL

Share how you each went about integrating last week's chapter into your life and practice. After reflecting on this chapter, what is one personal change you will make this week to partner with God in His plan of renewal? Share with the group, which will keep each other accountable next week.

_____

_____

_____

_____

_____

_____

CONTEND IN PRAYER

What is God asking you to cry out and contend for this week? Contend in prayer for renewal together.

CHAPTER 8: WHY THE CHURCH NEEDS RENEWAL
Embracing Hot Orthodoxy and Vital Christianity

WHAT KEY THINGS DID I LEARN FROM THIS CHAPTER?

1. _____

_____

_____

_____

_____

2. _____

_____

_____

_____

_____

3. _____

_____

_____

_____

_____

4. _____

_____

_____

_____

_____

5. _____

_____

_____

_____

_____

REFLECTIONS AND GROUP LEARNING – Discuss as a group.

What is one renewal principle that you learned in this week's reading? Each person shares one principle that has been discovered.

_____

_____

_____

_____

PARTNERING WITH GOD IN RENEWAL

Share how you each went about integrating last week's chapter into your life and practice. After reflecting on this chapter, what is one personal change you will make this week to partner with God in His plan of renewal? Share with the group, which will keep each other accountable next week.

_____

_____

_____

_____

_____

_____

_____

CONTEND IN PRAYER

What is God asking you to cry out and contend for this week? Contend in prayer for renewal together.

CHAPTER 9: PREPARING FOR RENEWAL
Breaking Down before Building Up

WHAT KEY THINGS DID I LEARN FROM THIS CHAPTER?

1. _____

_____

_____

_____

_____

2. _____

_____

_____

_____

_____

3. _____

_____

_____

_____

_____

4. _____

_____

_____

_____

_____

5. _____

_____

_____

_____

_____

REFLECTIONS AND GROUP LEARNING – Discuss as a group.

What is one renewal principle that you learned in this week's reading? Each person shares one principle that has been discovered.

_____

_____

_____

_____

PARTNERING WITH GOD IN RENEWAL

Share how you each went about integrating last week's chapter into your life and practice. After reflecting on this chapter, what is one personal change you will make this week to partner with God in His plan of renewal? Share with the group, which will keep each other accountable next week.

_____

_____

_____

_____

_____

_____

_____

CONTEND IN PRAYER

What is God asking you to cry out and contend for this week? Contend in prayer for renewal together.

CHAPTER 10: FROM CONSUMING TO CONTENDING
The Sacrificial, Risk-Taking, Responsibility-Embracing Posture of Renewal

WHAT KEY THINGS DID I LEARN FROM THIS CHAPTER?

1. _____

_____

_____

_____

_____

2. _____

_____

_____

_____

_____

3. _____

_____

_____

_____

_____

4. _____

_____

_____

_____

_____

5. _____

_____

_____

_____

_____

REFLECTIONS AND GROUP LEARNING – Discuss as a group.

What is one renewal principle that you learned in this week's reading? Each person shares one principle that has been discovered.

_____

_____

_____

_____

PARTNERING WITH GOD IN RENEWAL

Share how you each went about integrating last week's chapter into your life and practice. After reflecting on this chapter, what is one personal change you will make this week to partner with God in His plan of renewal? Share with the group, which will keep each other accountable next week.

_____

_____

_____

_____

_____

_____

_____

CONTEND IN PRAYER

What is God asking you to cry out and contend for this week? Contend in prayer for renewal together.

CHAPTER 11: REPATTERNING FOR RENEWAL
Cultivating Faith in the West's Secular Mega-Temple

WHAT KEY THINGS DID I LEARN FROM THIS CHAPTER?

1. _____

_____

_____

_____

_____

2. _____

_____

_____

_____

_____

3. _____

_____

_____

_____

_____

4. _____

_____

_____

_____

5. _____

_____

_____

_____

REFLECTIONS AND GROUP LEARNING – Discuss as a group.

What is one renewal principle that you learned in this week's reading? Each person shares one principle that has been discovered.

_____

_____

_____

_____

PARTNERING WITH GOD IN RENEWAL

Share how you each went about integrating last week's chapter into your life and practice. After reflecting on this chapter, what is one personal change you will make this week to partner with God in His plan of renewal? Share with the group, which will keep each other accountable next week.

_____

_____

_____

_____

_____

_____

_____

CONTEND IN PRAYER

What is God asking you to cry out and contend for this week? Contend in prayer for renewal together.

CHAPTER 12: REMNANTS: THE CELLS OF RENEWAL
How Small Groups Lead to Big Renewals

WHAT KEY THINGS DID I LEARN FROM THIS CHAPTER?

1. _____

_____

_____

_____

_____

2. _____

_____

_____

_____

_____

3. _____

_____

_____

_____

_____

4. _____

_____

_____

_____

_____

5. _____

_____

_____

_____

_____

REFLECTIONS AND GROUP LEARNING – Discuss as a group.

What is one renewal principle that you learned in this week's reading? Each person shares one principle that has been discovered.

_____

_____

_____

_____

PARTNERING WITH GOD IN RENEWAL

Share how you each went about integrating last week's chapter into your life and practice. After reflecting on this chapter, what is one personal change you will make this week to partner with God in His plan of renewal? Share with the group, which will keep each other accountable next week.

_____

_____

_____

_____

_____

_____

_____

CONTEND IN PRAYER

What is God asking you to cry out and contend for this week? Contend in prayer for renewal together.

CHAPTER 13: WHEN RENEWAL GOES VIRAL
How Form and Fire Empower Revival

WHAT KEY THINGS DID I LEARN FROM THIS CHAPTER?

1. _____
_____
_____
_____
_____

2. _____
_____
_____
_____
_____

3. _____
_____
_____
_____
_____

4. _____
_____
_____
_____
_____

5. _____
_____
_____
_____
_____

REFLECTIONS AND GROUP LEARNING – Discuss as a group.

What is one renewal principle that you learned in this week's reading? Each person shares one principle that has been discovered.

_____

_____

_____

_____

PARTNERING WITH GOD IN RENEWAL

Share how you each went about integrating last week's chapter into your life and practice. After reflecting on this chapter, what is one personal change you will make this week to partner with God in His plan of renewal? Share with the group, which will keep each other accountable next week.

_____

_____

_____

_____

_____

_____

CONTEND IN PRAYER

What is God asking you to cry out and contend for this week? Contend in prayer for renewal together.

Acknowledgments

Thanks: The Moody team for all their hard work. Trudi for walking the trails of revival with me, the Sayers clan, and Red Church family. The endless conversations over the last two years with friends, leaders, believers, listeners of *This Cultural Moment*, all hungering for a move of God in our time. A remnant is forming, a hunger is growing. Time to contend in prayer.

Notes

INTRODUCTION: CREATING A RENEWAL CELL

1. Ronald Rolheiser, *The Shattered Lantern: Rediscovering a Felt Presence of God* (New York: Crossroads, 2004), 52.

2. Douglas Hyde, *Dedication and Leadership: Learning from the Communists* (Notre Dame, IN: Notre Dame Press, 1966), 33.

3. Hyde, *Dedication and Leadership*, 57.

4. Michael Green, *30 Years That Changed the World: A Fresh Look at the Book of Acts* (Nottingham, UK: IVP, 1993), 116.

5. Green, *30 Years That Changed the World*, 213.

CHAPTER 1: THE SECULARIST RENEWAL MYTH

1. Ted Turnau, *Popologetics: Popular Culture in Christian Perspective* (Phillipsburg, NJ: P & R books, 2012), 13.

2. For more on how secular Western culture does this see Dallas Willard, *Knowing Christ Today: Why We Can Trust Spiritual Knowledge* (New York: HarperCollins, 2009).

3. Christopher Dawson, *Progress and Religion* (New York: Image Books, 1960), 14.

4. James Burns, *The Laws of Revival* (Philadelphia: Calvary Chapel of Philadelphia, 2013), 15.

5. See Peter Gay, *The Enlightenment: The Rise in Modern Paganism* (New York: Norton, 1966).

6. John R. Hinde, *Jacob Burckhardt and the Crisis of Modernity* (Montreal: McGill-Queens University Press, 2000), 24.

7. Thomas Paine quoted in Yuval Levin, *The Great Debate: Edmund Burke, Thomas Paine, and the Birth of Right and Left* (New York: Basic Books, 2014), 48.

8. John Micklethwait and Adrian Woolridge, *God Is Back: How the Global Revival of Faith Is Changing the World* (New York: Penguin, 2009), 17–18.

9. "How Australians Born Overseas Are Bucking the Millennial Stereotype," News.com.au, July 26, 2018, https://www.news.com.au/lifestyle/real-life/news-life/how-australians-born-overseas-are-bucking-the-millennial-stereotype/news-story/53a741374aaadcbcb062f448f95ddfc0.

10. Mike Stobbe, "Life Expectancy Will Likely Decline for Third Straight Year," Bloomberg, May 23, 2018, https://www.bloomberg.com/news/articles/2018-05-23/with-death-rate-up-us-life-expectancy-is-likely-down-again; Jimmy Nsubuga, "Life Expectancy Is Now Falling in Britain," Metro, January 18, 2018, https://metro.co.uk/2018/01/18/life-expectancy-now-falling-britain-7241492/.

Chapter 2: The Renewal Pattern

1. Peter M. Senge, *The Fifth Discipline: The Art and Practice of The Learning Organisation* (Milsons Point, NSW: Random House Australia, 1990), 12.

2. See Albert C. Outler, *Evangelism & Theology in the Wesleyan Spirit* (Nashville: Discipleship Resources, 2000), chapter 3.

3. Tim Keller, *Center Church: Doing Balanced, Gospel-Centered Ministry in Your City* (Grand Rapids: Zondervan, 2012), 55.

4. Joshua Ryan Butler, *The Skeletons in God's Closet: The Mercy of Hell, the Surprise of Judgment, the Hope of Holy War* (Nashville: Thomas Nelson, 2014), 78.

Chapter 3: Crisis—The Gateway to Renewal

1. George G. Hunter III, *To Spread the Power: Church Growth in the Wesleyan Spirit* (Nashville: Abingdon Press, 1987), 84–85.

2. William Bridges, *Managing Transitions: Making the Most of Change* (Cambridge, MA: Da Capo Press, 1991), 4–5.

3. Terry B. Walling, *Stuck!: Navigating the Transitions of Life and Leadership*, revised and updated (Chico, CA: Leader Breakthru, 2015), 13.

4. John P. Kotter, *Leading Change* (Boston: Harvard Business Review Press, 1996), 46.

5. Wilbert R. Shenk, *Changing Frontiers of Mission* (Maryknoll, NY: Orbis Books, 1999), 124; quoted in Bill Jackson, *The Quest for the Radical Middle: A History of the Vineyard* (Cape Town, South Africa: Vineyard International Publishing, 1999), 255.

6. James Burns, *The Laws of Revival* (Philadelphia: Calvary Chapel of Philadelphia, 2013), 29.

7. Charles Malik, *Christ and Crisis* (Grand Rapids: Acton Institute, 2015), 2.

8. Malik, *Christ and Crisis*, 1–2.

9. Lesslie Newbigin, *Honest Religion for Secular Man* (London: Bloomsbury, 1966), 76.

10. Quote and story from Nassim Nicholas Taleb, *Antifragile: Things That Gain from Disorder* (New York: Random House, 2012), 393.

CHAPTER 4: FROM DISSATISFACTION TO HOLY DISCONTENT

1. George G. Hunter III, *To Spread the Power: Church Growth in the Wesleyan Spirit* (Nashville: Abingdon Press, 1987), 84.

2. James Burns, *The Laws of Revival* (Philadelphia: Calvary Chapel of Philadelphia, 2013), 29.

3. See Dan P. McAdams, *The Redemptive Self: Stories Americans Live By* (New York: Oxford University Press, 2013).

4. See Philip Cushman, *Constructing the Self, Constructing America: A Cultural History of Psychotherapy* (Reading, MA: Addison-Wesley, 1995).

5. Thomas De Zengotita, *Mediated: How the Media Shape the World Around You* (London: Bloomsbury, 2005), 11.

6. Michael Wilcock, *The Message of Psalms 1–72* (Nottingham, UK: IVP, 2001), 21.

7. Hendrik Berkhof, *Christ and the Powers* (Scottsdale, PA: Herald Press, 1962), 28.

8. Donella H. Meadows, *Thinking in Systems: A Primer* (White River Junction, VT: Chelsea Green Publishing Company, 2008), 11.

9. The Bible Project, "Shalom / Peace," video, https://thebibleproject.com/videos/shalom-peace/.

10. Joseph O'Connor and Ian McDermott, *The Art of Systems Thinking: Essential Skills for Creativity and Problem Solving* (London: Thorsons, 1997), 19.

11. Byung-Chul Han, *Psychopolitics: Neoliberalism and New Technologies of Power* (London: Verso, 2017), iBook edition, 23.

CHAPTER 5: RENEWAL IN AN ANXIOUS CULTURE

1. Edwin H. Friedman, *A Failure of Nerve: Leadership in the Age of the Quick Fix* (New York: Church Publishing, 1999), 59.

2. Friedman, *A Failure of Nerve*, 61.

3. Friedman, *A Failure of Nerve*, 65.

4. Friedman, *Failure of Nerve*, 14–15.

5. Friedman, *A Failure of Nerve*, 15–16.

6. See Hugh Evans Hopkins, *Charles Simeon of Cambridge* (London: Hodder and Stoughton, 1977).

7. John Piper, *The Roots of Endurance* (Wheaton, IL: Crossway, 2002), 94.

8. Hopkins, *Charles Simeon of Cambridge*, 29.

9. See Pete Greig, *Dirty Glory: Go Where Your Best Prayers Take You* (London: Hodder & Stoughton, 2016).

10. Friedman, *A Failure of Nerve*, 18.

11. Friedman, *A Failure of Nerve*, 20.

12. Friedman, *A Failure of Nerve*, 19.

13. Henry and Richard Blackaby, Claude King, *Experiencing God: Knowing and Doing the Will of God* (Nashville: B&H, 2008), 106.

CHAPTER 6: SECULARISM VS. THE PRESENCE

1. Kevin J. Vanhoozer, *The Drama of Doctrine: A Canonical-Linguistic Approach to Christian Theology* (Louisville: Westminster John Knox Press, 2005), 3.

2. John H. Walton, *The Lost World of Genesis One: Ancient Cosmology and the Origins Debate* (Downers Grove, IL: IVP, 2009), loc. 708–12, Kindle.

3. John H. Walton, *Ancient Near Eastern Thought and the Old Testament: Introducing the Conceptual World of the Hebrew Bible* (Grand Rapids: Baker, 2018), 88.

4. G. K. Beale, *The Temple and the Church's Mission: A Biblical Theology of the Dwelling Place of God* (Leicester, UK: Apollos, 2004), 59.

5. Beale, *The Temple and the Church's Mission*, 59

6. Walton, *The Lost World of Genesis One*, loc. 798.

7. Walton, *The Lost World of Genesis One*, loc. 798.

8. Walton, *The Lost World of Genesis One*, loc. 803.

9. Beale, *The Temple and the Church's Mission*, 85.

10. N. T. Wright, *Paul: A Biography* (New York: HarperCollins, 2018), 48.

11. Beale, *The Temple and the Church's Mission*, 48.

12. Peter J. Leithart, *Delivered from the Elements of the World: Atonement, Justification, Mission* (Downers Grove, IL: IVP, 2016), 76.

13. See J. Ryan Lister, *The Presence of God: Its Place in the Storyline of Scripture and the Story of Our Lives* (Wheaton, IL: Crossway, 2015), chapter 4.

14. Lister, *The Presence of God*, 92.

CHAPTER 7: RENEWAL TO THE ENDS OF THE EARTH

1. Peter J. Leithart, *Delivered from the Elements of the World: Atonement, Justification, Mission* (Downers Grove, IL: IVP, 2016), 77.

2. J. Ryan Lister, *The Presence of God: Its Place in the Storyline of Scripture and the Story of Our Lives* (Wheaton, IL: Crossway, 2015), 256.

3. Lister, *The Presence of God*, 257.

4. Leithart, *Delivered from the Elements of the World*, 77.

5. Anthony J. Kelly, *Upward: Faith, Church, and the Ascension of Christ* (Collegeville, MN: Liturgical Press, 2010), 8.

6. Kelly, *Upward*, 9.

7. Andrew Murray, in Louis Gifford Parkhurst Jr., *The Believer's Secret of the Abiding Presence* (Minneapolis: Bethany House, 2012), iBook edition, 18.

CHAPTER 8: WHY THE CHURCH NEEDS RENEWAL

1. Richard F. Lovelace, *Dynamics of Spiritual Life: An Evangelical Theology of Renewal* (Downers Grove, IL: IVP Academic, 1979), 72.

2. Howard A. Snyder, *Signs of the Spirit: How God Reshapes the Church* (Grand Rapids: Academic Books, 1989), 23.

3. Stuart Piggin, *Spirit, Word and World: Evangelicalism in Australia* (Brunswick East, Victoria: Acorn Press, 2012), xiii. Piggin uses Spirit, Word, and World to describe evangelicalism at its best, especially in an Australian context. This said, I think that the definition works well for vital Christianity.

4. Lovelace, *Dynamics of Spiritual Life*, 73.

5. See D. Martyn Lloyd-Jones, *Joy Unspeakable: The Baptism with the Holy Spirit* (Eastbourne: Kingsway, 1984), 112–13.

6. John Wesley, *John Wesley's Journal* (London: Hodder & Stoughton, 1993), 56.

7. Quoted in Peter Kreeft, *Christianity for Modern Pagans: Pascal's Pensées* (San Francisco: Ignatius, 1993), 325.

8. Dallas Willard, *The Divine Conspiracy: Rediscovering Our Hidden Life in God* (London: HarperCollins, 1998), 50.

9. Lovelace, *Dynamics of Spiritual Life*, 205.

10. Lewis Drummond, *Spurgeon: Prince of Preachers* (Grand Rapids: Kregel, 1992), 268.

11. See chapter 3 of Victor Cha, *The Impossible State: North Korea, Past and Future* (London: Random House, 2012).

12. William J. Abraham, *The Logic of Renewal* (London: SPCK, 2003), 4.

13. Abraham, *The Logic of Renewal*, 144.

CHAPTER 9: PREPARING FOR RENEWAL

1. L. P. Hartley, *The Go-Between* (1953; repr., New York: The New York Review of Books, 2002), 17.

2. Ernest Hemmingway, *A Moveable Feast* (1964; repr., New York: Scribner, 2003), 29.

3. George M. Marsden, *Jonathan Edwards: A Life* (New Haven, CT: Yale University Press, 2003), 159.

4. Martyn Llyod-Jones, *Revival: Can We Make It Happen?* (Basingstoke, UK: Marshall Pickering, 1986), 130.

5. Gregory of Nyssa in *Devotional Classics: Selected Readings for Individuals and Groups*, Richard J. Foster and James Bryan Smith, eds. (San Francisco: Harper, 1990).

6. James I. Packer, *God in Our Midst: Seeking and Receiving Ongoing Revival* (Ann Arbor, MI: Vine Books, 1987), 26.

7. Quoted in Henry and Richard Blackaby, Claude King, *Fresh Encounter: God's Pattern For Spiritual Renewal* (Nashville: B&H Publishing, 2009), 165.

8. Arthur Wallis, *In the Day of Thy Power: The Scriptural Principles of Revival* (1956; repr., Fort Washington, PA: CLC Publications, 2010), 114.

9. M. Basilea Schlink, *Repentance: The Joy-Filled Life* (Darmstadt, Germany: Kanaan, 1992), 15.

10. This is the great life mantra of my friend and mentor Terry Walling and one of the most fruitful truths he has spoken into my life.

11. Richard F. Lovelace, *Dynamics of Spiritual Life: An Evangelical Theology of Renewal* (Downers Grove, IL: IVP Academic, 1979), 65.

CHAPTER 10: FROM CONSUMING TO CONTENDING

1. Tim Herrera, "How to Beat F.O.B.O., From the Author Who Coined It," *New York Times*, July 30, 2018, https://www.nytimes.com/2018/07/30/smarter-living/how-to-beat-fobo-from-the-expert-who-coined-it.html.

2. John Townsend, *The Entitlement Cure: Finding Success in Doing Hard Things The Right Way* (Grand Rapids: Zondervan, 2015), 50.

3. Nassim Nicholas Taleb, *Antifragile: Things That Gain from Disorder* (New York: Random House, 2012), 375.

4. Taleb, *Antifragile*, 378, 376.

5. Edwin H. Friedman, *A Failure of Nerve: Leadership in the Age of the Quick Fix* (New York: Church Publishing, 1999), 206.

6. Friedman, *A Failure of Nerve*, 206.

7. Arthur Wallis, *In the Day of Thy Power: The Scriptural Principles of Revival* (1956; repr., Fort Washington, PA: CLC Publications, 2010), 202.

8. Michael S. Heiser, *Supernatural: What the Bible Teaches about the Unseen World—and Why It Matters* (Bellingham, WA: Lexham Press, 2015), 139.

9. Michael S. Heiser, *Supernatural*, 138.

CHAPTER 11: REPATTERNING FOR RENEWAL

1. E. H. Gombrich, *The Story of Art* (Oxford, UK: Phaidon, 1989), 126.

2. Daniel Goleman, *Focus: The Hidden Driver of Excellence* (New York: Harper, 2013), 24.

3. Alexander Schmemann, *For the Life of the World: Sacraments and Orthodoxy* (Crestwood, NY: St Vladimir's Seminary Press, 1963), 15.

4. Schmemann, *For the Life of the World*, 17.

5. Schmemann, *For the Life of the World*, 17.

6. James K. A. Smith, *You Are What You Love: The Spiritual Power of Habit* (Grand Rapids: Brazos, 2016), 11.

7. Smith, *You Are What You Love*, 12.

8. Dallas Willard, *The Spirit of the Disciplines: Understanding How God Changes Lives* (London: Hodder & Stoughton, 1988), 52.

9. Tom Wright, *Virtue Reborn* (London: SPCK, 2010), 72.

10. Willard, *The Spirit of the Disciplines*, 67.

11. Abraham Heschel, *The Sabbath: Its Meaning for Modern Man* (New York: Farrar, Straus and Giroux, 2005).

CHAPTER 12: REMNANTS—THE CELLS OF RENEWAL

1. Quoted in Howard A. Snyder, *Signs of the Spirit: How God Reshapes the Church* (Grand Rapids: Academic Books, 1989), 83.

2. Gerald McDermott, "Theology of the Remnant," April 14, 2015, *The Northampton Seminar* (blog), http://www.patheos.com/blogs/northamptonseminar/2015/04/14/theology-of-the-remnant/.

3. Richard F. Lovelace, *Dynamics of Spiritual Life: An Evangelical Theology of Renewal* (Downers Grove, IL: IVP Academic, 1979), 207.

4. McDermott, "Theology of the Remnant."

5. "Research: Only 17% of Christians Actually Have a Biblical Worldview," *Relevant* magazine, May 11, 2017, https://relevantmagazine.com/slice/research-only-17-of-christians-actually-have-a-biblical-worldview/. The definition of a biblical worldview was this statement: "believing that absolute moral truth exists; the Bible is totally accurate in all of the principles it

teaches; Satan is considered to be a real being or force, not merely symbolic; a person cannot earn their way into Heaven by trying to be good or do good works; Jesus Christ lived a sinless life on earth; and God is the all-knowing, all-powerful creator of the world who still rules the universe today."

6. I first heard the metaphor of a worm given by Graham Cooke in a sermon.

7. See Howard A. Snyder, *Signs of the Spirit: How God Reshapes the Church* (Grand Rapids: Academic Books, 1989), 35.

8. Martyn Lloyd-Jones, *Revival* (Wheaton, IL: Crossway, 1987), 13.

9. Lloyd-Jones, *Revival*, 13.

10. Lloyd-Jones, *Revival*, 19.

11. Lloyd-Jones, *Revival*, 20.

12. Richard J. Foster, *Prayer: Finding the Heart's True Home* (London: Hodder and Stoughton, 1992), 7.

13. Alan Kreider, *The Patient Ferment of the Early Church: The Improbable Rise of Christianity in the Roman Empire* (Grand Rapids: Baker, 2016), 12.

CHAPTER 13: WHEN RENEWAL GOES VIRAL

1. John O'Donohue in *The Confession of Saint Patrick* (New York: Image Books, 1998), ix.

2. Louis Gougand, quoted in George G. Hunter III, *The Celtic Way of Evangelism: How Christianity Can Reach the West . . . Again* (Nashville: Abingdon, 2010), 11.

3. Mike Breen, *Leading Kingdom Movements: The "Everyman" Notebook on How to Change the World* (Pawley's Island, SC: 3DM Publishing, 2013), 184.

4. Stuart Piggin, *Firestorm of the Lord: The History of and Prospects for Revival in the Church and the World* (Carlisle, UK: Paternoster, 2000), 105.

5. Anthony Giddens, *The Consequences of Modernity* (Cambridge: Polity, 1990), 19.

6. Peter L. Berger, *The Heretical Imperative: Contemporary Possibilities of Religious Affirmation* (Garden City, NY: Anchor Press, 1979), 30.

7. Parag Khanna, *Connectography: Mapping the Future of Global Civilization* (New York: Random House, 2016), xvi–xvii.

8. Mark A. Noll, *The Rise of Evangelicalism: The Age of Edwards, Whitefield and the Wesleys* (Nottingham, UK: IVP, 2004), 144.

9. See Tim Keller, *Center Church: Doing Balanced, Gospel-Centered Ministry in Your City* (Grand Rapids: Zondervan, 2012), 315.

10. See Leonard Sweet, *The Greatest Story Never Told: Revive Us Again* (Nashville: Abingdon Press, 2012), xxi.

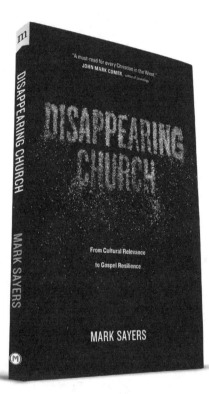

DOES THE WORLD MAKE YOU DIZZY?

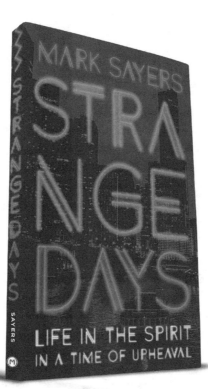

MOODY
Publishers®

*From the Word **to** Life®*

In these crazy times, we can all benefit from someone who understands culture yet trusts the Bible. Mark Sayers, a gifted cultural analyst, is that person. In *Strange Days* he combines his biblical knowledge, curious mind, and pastoral heart to help Christians slow down, get their bearings, and follow God with wisdom in this wild world.

978-0-8024-1573-8 | also available as an eBook

CAN'T FIND NO SATISFACTION?

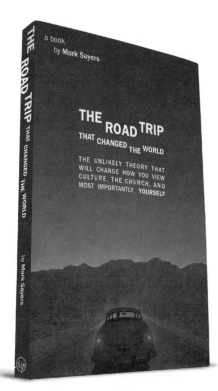